Hope
Healing
Spirit

Strength, Solace and Self-Advocacy for the Bipolar Community

HOPE
HEALING
SPIRIT

*Strength, Solace and Self-Advocacy
for the Bipolar Community*

Dr. Kay Bernard

Copyright © 2016 Dr. Kay Bernard

All rights reserved.

ISBN-13: 978-1500155322
ISBN-10: 150015532

About the cover

The innate force of hope, the consistent attention to healing and the comfort of spirit come together as the three legs of a birthing chair, historical furniture to aid women giving birth. This chair, today called the "tribal chair," had legs set in the form of a triangle, tilted toward the back and with holes to give a woman a place to put her feet. The midwife faces the woman, who is in a strategic position to push out her baby. In 1973 I bought such a chair in Tanzania. For me, it is a symbol of women through the centuries bringing forth new life. Three legs held up these women. So it is with the three foundations of birthing a quality of life: much "pushing" on the part of the person with bipolar disorder, family and friends who stand by with compassion and support, and skilled professionals who help a person to move from the destruction of the disorder to stability achieved through medications, talk therapy, support people and emergency care.

For Terrence Patrick Thomas Larkin
No greater husband than he

Contents

Acknowledgements	ii
Introduction	iv

Hope
Don & Ji-Young	3
George & Helen	7
Steven	10
Andrew	14
Meditation	18
My Story	24

Healing
Emily	29
Joseph	34
Beatrice & Harold	38
Hank & Stone	42
Kisha	47
Laura	51
Meditation	56
My Story	72

Spirit
Ann & Charlie	77
Child	82
Leah	86
Meditation	90
My Story	95

About the Author	99

Acknowledgments

In Shakespeare's play *Macbeth*, Lady Macbeth notices a red spot on her hand, a foreshadowing of future bloodshed. Scared and angry she screams, "Out, damned spot! Out, I say!. . ." Her words characterize the frequent instruction of my editor, **DR. BARBARA F. LUEBKE**, Professor Emerita of Journalism at the University of Rhode Island. She is the author of several books and many articles, and in retirement is a freelance editor. Without her vast editorial skills, abiding patience, deep rivers of compassion and jaunty humor, this book would have remained a "next year" on my part. Now it is a reality. My gratefulness is everlasting.

When I spoke with **DR. JEAN MORRIS TRUMBAUR**, my thesis faculty advisor and cherished friend, she always said, "You are and will make a significant contribution to people with bipolar disorder and support people." Without her unwavering faith in me, this book would have remained fodder for conversation.

Writing for public consumption fills my brain with negative self-talk. I relied on nine women I call **SISTERS** to help me fill the spaces between peace and self-doubt. They would heal my heart. Each unselfishly offered a listening presence, belly laughs, successful distractions, limitless affirmations and a continuous bucket of forgiveness. These unselfish "sisters" -- Trisha A., BFL, Deb D., Kaia L., Mary Jane L., Gily M., Karla M., Myrle M. and Barbara W. -- embraced me with love.

UNION CONGREGATIONAL CHURCH in Hackensack, Minnesota, taught me the practice of spiritual hospitality. Without hesitation, they gave me, a stranger, all the resources I needed to write. My hours varied, so they gave me a key to the church. They accommodated my physical health problem, allowing me to be included in activities – the fiber group my most cherished one. They even allowed my dog, Miss Gerty, to join me when I worked. This church blessed me. Thank you.

To the people with bipolar disorder and the support people who shared their stories with me, I am honored to hold your trust. The best illustration of my appreciation is a Charles Schulz comic strip from the early 1970s. Snoopy admits to himself that he ruined his best friend Woodstock's party. Woodstock had invited a cute little bird he was in love with, but he had no time with her because Snoopy had talked her ear off. Woodstock was brokenhearted and sent Snoopy a bill of $6 for a broken heart. Snoopy, clutching the bill in one paw and Woodstock in the other, uttered, "Oh, Woodstock, my little friend of friends. Don't you realize your heart is worth much more than $6?!!" Oh, my **BIPOLAR COMMUNITY**, know that to me you are worth much more than a million dollars. You have enriched my life. I hope this book does the same for you.

Introduction

Throughout these last several years, when someone has asked me what kind of work I do, my answer has been, "I work with people with bipolar disorder and their loved ones to enhance hope, healing and their spirituality." Many lift an eyebrow, as if they have no idea what I am talking about. Others pause, show polite interest and then say something like, "That's a heavy topic." Some, stuck in silence, nod their heads in recognition of the need for such work, whether for personal or professional reasons. Occasionally, a person quietly begins telling me a story of vulnerabilities, aloneness, destroyed relationships and grief. Then, with hesitation, some tell of attempted suicides. Each seeks from me validation of their tough life with bipolar disorder. Support people also share stories of someone who struggles with the disorder or another mental illness. These stories typically revolve around a person who scares, hurts or blames them. Then the support people explain why they maintain the relationship. They typically want validation of their decisions and recognition of their tough life.

People's stories bring to light twin curses: stigma and shame. These twins have been around a very long time. In the Bible's Old Testament, someone with leprosy, typically described as a person with sores and demonically possessed, was considered "unclean." She was excluded – separated -- from any contact outside of those like herself. Two thousand years later, in Jesus' ministry, those who were demonically possessed or were judged to have leprosy were not to be near Jesus. But he welcomed the outcasts and healed them.

For those who were not healed and remained captive to inward violent voices and outward bizarre behaviors, the questions "Why me, God? Where are you in my suffering?" would be cynically -- and frequently -- asked. The expected answer -- always silence. The only imaginable explanation for God's lack of compassion was that God had singled them out for suffering. They were born flawed and therefore unacceptable to God; they were despicable and worthy of abandonment.

These questions and the absence of easy answers led me to enter a seminary to wrestle with them and finally to write a thesis, "In God's Own Image: Spiritual Resources for People with Bipolar Disorder and Those Who Care For Them." I used the creation stories from the first chapters in the book of Genesis (New Revised Standard Edition) as my primary resource, along with my own 1991 diagnosis of bipolar disorder.

My post-1991 life -- managing a major health issue -- led me into the complex world of medications. My first medication worked well, but eventually I had to add another for side effects, and on and on throughout the years. I regularly met with my psychiatrist, therapist and primary physician. I attended Depression-Bipolar Support Groups. And I went off medications three times -- very bad decisions.

I have felt stigma. I have felt shame. I have obtained and maintained professional positions, given the blessings of hypomania. I have lost most of them from the curse of hypomania and depression. I have embraced husband and children and deeply hurt them. I have found rich relationships and bruised many of them. Yet the question "Why me, God?" has *not* troubled me. "Why does God allow so much suffering by people who were born with a lifelong illness?" -- that has been my question.

I know I stand on the shoulders of heroes who lived and died with this disorder never knowing any freedom, only fear, anger and punishment. Their families and friends also have lived with the twins. Because of the questions asked of God, and the twins that destroy people's freedom, I felt compelled to look at God first in order to diminish the power of stigma and shame.

To get at spiritual issues, opinions and beliefs from those most affected by bipolar disorder, for my doctoral thesis forty people confidentially answered questions based on thirteen fictional stories. Information gleaned from those who responded -- thirteen professionals, ten people with bipolar disorder and seventeen support people – is reflected throughout this book.

Each story included a character with bipolar disorder and a family member or friend. Symptoms and the consequential behaviors drove the stories. After each story came a segment offering commentary on it, a spiritual issue that arose from the story and a prayer offered by one of the characters. For this book, I have slightly revised the stories and added meditations about Hope, Healing and Spirit. Each section ends with my own related story. It is important to note that the stories that precede each meditation are not exclusive to it. For example, the story of Hank could have appeared in both Hope and Spirit.

Before you read further, a couple comments on terminology are in order. Over the last several years, "bipolar person" has gone out of use in recognition that a person is more than his or her disease. Thus a simple sentence such as "Mary assists her bipolar friend, John" is frowned upon because it sends the message that John's disorder singularly defines him. But describing people more fully can lead to cumbersome prose. For example: "Mary, a caregiver for John, a person with bipolar disorder, met for coffee with Robert, a person with depression, and his support person Mike." When this structure is repeated a few times, the intentional message can get lost given all the descriptive terminology. This example of cumbersome wording, however, does signal an essential fact -- people with mental illness are more than their disorder.

I choose the cumbersome language to give John and Mike the freedom to be complete people. I trust that readers will plow through the verbiage to understand the message. Finally, the terms "caregiver" and "support person" are used interchangeably, and neither is meant to narrowly define the individual providing care or support. Other terms that indicate support -- such as "loved one," "one who loves a person with bipolar" and "friend who offers help" -- also are used.

A new term, Bipolar Community, is used on the cover of the book and numerous times within its pages. The term brings together under one umbrella doctors, therapists, social workers, spiritual confidants, patients/clients, support people and local and national organizations providing resources to all the groups and those interested in bipolar disorder. Most importantly, belonging to a community enhances the feeling that one is not alone in dealing with a serious health issue. Community -- coming together -- attacks stigma and shame.

My hope in writing this book is that readers will recognize themselves in some of the stories, experience validation of their struggles and lean on the mediations on hope, healing and spirit to strengthen their life journey with a mental disease that affects every decision facing those with the disorder as well as their support system.

Hope

DON & JI-YOUNG

The Story

Don has managed his bipolar disorder for years. He consistently takes his medicine and regularly visits his doctor. Both he and Ji-Young, his wife of two years, attend a bipolar depression support group several times a year at their church. Don hopes the group will help Ji-Young understand that his brain disorder is just that, not a character disorder. Ji-Young emotionally hides during these meetings because sharing such personal information exposes her family to public shame. She would rather stay at home, but she recognizes that these meetings help Don to stay healthy.

Don enjoys Ji-Young and the three children from his first marriage. He makes time to attend his children's softball and lacrosse games. People describe him as "laid back." As a real estate advisor, he keeps track of the housing market. Before a recent downturn, he made a good living. Lately, several articles, web sites and professional magazines have reported that restoration of the housing market may take up to five years. This makes Don nervous because he doesn't have the money to wait that long for a recovery.

Don's worries intensify. He speaks fearfully to his colleagues. At home sleep eludes him, family finances scare him and interest in the children has waned. He misses more of his kids' games and becomes short with Ji-Young. When she questions him, Don snaps, "If you had the responsibility of providing for this family, you would worry too. I'm doing the best that I can. I would appreciate a little support instead of criticism." Ji-Young shies away.

The family attends their biennial extended-family picnic. Don uncharacteristically argues, mocks and ridicules several favorite relatives. The gathering gets ugly. No one speaks on the ride home. Once there, Don immediately goes to his computer. He races from web site to web site. A site with a link, "No Hope; No Miracles," grabs his attention. He opens it to see two gladiators fighting. One wears a breastplate with a cross; the other a breastplate with a neon 6. Words in large orange print read, "Help God Defeat Satan." The action is real, the intensity raw, the words mesmerizing. Racing, scary thoughts buzz through Don's mind: "What if God doesn't win this war!" He falls to his knees gushing out words that may strengthen him. At two in the morning he grabs the phone and calls all the guys in his Bible study group. He pleads with them to pray for God's victory.

Ji-Young hears the weeping and wailing downstairs. She resents Don's outbursts but has learned she must get him to safety. She lures him into the car and drives him to the emergency room.

Comments on the Story

Ji-Young, acting contrary to her cultural norms, supports Don in the manner he most requires. For many people, managing their bipolar disorder requires attention and support, but it is not their major focus every day. Additionally, many people with bipolar function undetected at work and with friends. Months or even years may pass with no noticeable episodes, as in Don's case. But when symptoms begin to erupt, the support person is usually the one to notice.

Typically, people's moods change with increased stress, which can ignite a hypomanic/manic or depressive mood. For Don, the fluidity of the housing market dramatically affected his income and his sense of personal security. He became anxious, argumentative and judgmental. Fear gripped him and no external information could steady him. He isolated himself from others and allowed his computer to become his best friend. He searched web sites day and night, looking to be comforted and separated from his feelings of impending doom.

In that state, he glanced at a web site that captured images of battle. This fight had no context. Don created his own story, which reflected a hidden religious belief: namely, that God and Satan use human vessels to fight for dominance. Don believes people must be alert to an impending battle and remain strong to allow God to win. But his church teaches that God is loving and merciful. No one in the congregation would believe that "laid back" Don could believe such nonsense.

Spiritual Reflection

Two opposing spiritual beings battling for supremacy within a person's body is a religious belief rarely found in twenty-first century churches. People with bipolar disorder may be more susceptible to this theology given their perception of God during hypomania and depression. When a person with bipolar feels high self-esteem mixed with intense energy and extreme confidence, a great God may be part of the ride. When despair, self-loathing and hopelessness dominate a bipolar life, God may be experienced as critical, judgmental and punishing. Within this dichotomy, fertile soil awaits for Don's confusion and vulnerability as to God's true nature.

The motif of God and Satan battling has ancient roots. When the book of Genesis was written thousands of years ago, neighboring cultures believed that gods battled for supremacy and humans were created to serve these various gods. The God found in the Bible, however, fought no other deity -- neither in the universe nor in humanity. People were birthed from the dust of a newly formed earth and God's own breath. This divine action uplifted humanity into a life with God. Satan already had lost the battle.

Don's Satan/God battle conducted within human skin makes sense given his vastly different images of God, depending on his mood. In most months, he knows a loving and merciful God. In the hospital, alone in silent darkness, an evil presence may creep into his mind and whisper in his ear.

Don's Prayer

Who are you, God? Sometimes you are my best friend and I feel you totally understand me; at other times, I feel as if Satan sat in the same room with me, laughing at you. I am sick and tired of this dance. Make up your mind. Sitting here in the hospital I hear people shouting at you, others crying. It's not right. I think of my church. You live there. But when I am here, I feel no tug from you. Don't get me wrong. I feel blessed to have Ji-Young's love and my family's endurance. But right now, I just want to clear up a couple of things. Are you and Satan on speaking terms or do I need to brace myself for another confrontation? Just beat him up and get rid of him. If you did, I wouldn't get so confused and so damn angry. Help me out here. Well, amen.

GEORGE & HELEN

George's Story
I think my garage is the best place in the world. Now I am working on designing a new car. I've tried several ideas. Crumbled papers nearly cover the floor. I get one idea and then a slight modification is necessary. I throw out the old paper and begin again, incorporating my new concept. I can see the car I'm trying to draw. It would look like a canoe on wheels, except wider. The electrical engine would sit in the front and the back section would be available for luggage and stuff. I can make it wide enough to carry two people. Maybe I could design it for four passengers. My car will grab a piece of the market that no one has yet addressed. Maybe we will become rich. I have had to run to the hardware store several times and would you believe it, I got a speeding ticket.

I went to my AA meeting last night. I was stellar. An idiot started telling a story of woe. Before he finished I knew what he was going to say so I finished his story out loud. No one came close to hitting the bullseye like I did. I gave plenty of advice; of course we aren't supposed to, but I was brilliant. I did get a little irritated about how slow people talked and when they added ridiculous comments. They don't appreciate me. Neither does my wife. She stops by the garage to bring the phone, food or my medicine but she never stops to admire my work.

Helen's Story
When George stops taking his medication it is not long before he gets into one of his "moods." He has not slept for three days and with the

passing of time he becomes unbearable to be around -- one mood after another. I get no rest. He acts so mean to me. Even when he becomes depressed and never leaves the couch, the hurt doesn't go away.

Sometimes I wish *he* would go away. I don't care how. He never knows how awful he treats me or how rude he is to others, including our adult son, Chris. I rarely see Chris because he doesn't want to be around his dad. I wish I could leave. George is so much like his brother Henry, who criticized everyone and then we would not see him for a while. I don't miss him. George doesn't make much money; he has lost several jobs. We scrape by for now, but he spends so much money on his crazy ideas. We have saved nothing for retirement, which is just a few years away. George's moods have ruined everything. I had hoped for a better life. It's too late. Nothing will change.

Comments on the Stories

Many people with bipolar disorder enjoy spending money, often a lot more than they can afford. Other people enjoy the thrill of being treated to some luxurious outing, never evaluating whether "Rich Papa" can afford the adventure. George believes he is going to be rich. Lots of money and the status it would provide motivate George to work day and night. He believes himself to be inventive, creative and a high-risk-taker. Grandiosity, lack of sleep and elevated self-esteem sent George into a manic episode that could last several weeks.

George is mean to his wife and their 30-year-old son, Chris. What Helen doesn't know is that her son drinks until he's drunk. Another secret Helen doesn't know is that George's brother Henry completed suicide. George protects Helen from news that he believes would deeply disturb her. He loves Helen, but the ravages of untreated bipolar disorder have ruined their marriage, financial security and quality of life.

Helen has spent decades trying to be supportive of George. She cooks, cleans, does the laundry and listens to George's "saving-the-world" ideas as well as his barroom songs. She tries to be a good wife, but her efforts feel futile.

Frequently, a person with bipolar disorder relies on a support person, typically a family member. The job is difficult, the responsibility immense. The support person watches for signs of mood changes and makes herself available for conversation, even advice. At times, she accompanies the loved one to doctors' appointments. Usually the role of support person is a burden, but she can't allow a spouse or child to destroy himself when preventative measures are available. With this arrangement, boundaries may be difficult to establish and maintain. The support person may watch just a bit too closely, ask too many questions or give too much advice. The person with bipolar may be appreciative or resentful, withdrawn or intrusive, usually insensitive to the worries that occupy this valuable support person. What will happen to George if Helen decides to leave the marriage? Neither has much of a support system, not even a church that can uplift them.

Spiritual Reflection

God provided Adam and Eve an idyllic life if only they would obey one rule: not to eat from the Tree of the Knowledge of Good and Evil. God offered the Israelites a full life if only they would cease worshipping idols. Jesus set people free of bondage so they could live a full life and celebrate healing miracles. New life, free of spiritual and physical bondage, became available and each person praised God for the miracle.

Helen and George are in bondage. With limited resources and with no extra gas, George and Helen attend AA and Al-Anon intermittently. They have memorized the step that reads, "Came to believe that a power greater than ourselves could restore us to sanity." Believing such a statement takes energy and desire. Now, none exists. Such a life dulls the imagination and eliminates hope. When one's life situation consumes all the energy of the family, God's healing presence is blocked. God wants a full life for Helen and George. After all, they are the descendants of God's chosen people.

Helen's Prayer

Where are you God? I've waited for months -- no, years -- to be loved by my husband and son. Neither wants me around. Maybe I don't want to be with them either. It's so hard to leave. I would have no money. I know you said, "Ask in my name." Well, I've done that for about 21 years. I still don't have anything. My neighbor is into you and she tells me "It's all in God's time." I think I'll be dead before your time comes around. I'll just leave it at that. Amen.

STEVEN

The Story

Dan Fletcher, the CEO of Marine Research, arrives a few hours before he is to be the master of ceremonies for Steven Murphy's retirement party. The two have worked together for more than twenty-five years, enjoyed family vacations and attend the same church. Dan wouldn't miss his friend and colleague's well-deserved party for anything.

Steven, on the other hand, paces the second-floor hallway of his colonial home. He is gripped by anxiety. Scuff marks on the floor tell the story of Steven's life of worry. He is in the "What if" mindset at this time because he will be the center of attention. He fantasizes, "What if John takes the mic and tells people about the time the staff gathered for their weekly meeting and I ranted about the one percent increase in personal business expenses? What if Kathleen shares the story about the time I entertained clients over dinner and told jokes and stories until the early morning?" Steven remembers dozens of such incidents. He prays that no one even knows the sexual harassment report that could have been made to HR. The "What ifs" stop when Joan, his wife of 37 years, calls out that she is nearly ready to leave. She expects an evening of tributes to Steven. She knows he was not a perfect corporate guy and isn't always a model husband, but he's an ethical man who always apologizes.

The evening begins with Dan sharing several stories about Steven's significant contributions to the company. He also talks about how their friendship has grown, especially through their involvement in the church group "Spiritual Seekers." Dan concludes by turning to Steven and saying, "You have been my colleague. Now I consider you my brother."

After Dan finishes his comments, Steven lifts his glass in recognition of Dan's kind words. In the back of his mind, however, he is asking himself, "What if I had told Dan that I live and work with bipolar disorder? Would I be sitting here now? Would I be considered his brother?"

Comments on the Story

Fear of being stigmatized – and its twin, shame -- is prevalent among those with bipolar. One of the high-risk decisions people face is whether to disclose or remain silent. Their family and friends must make the same decision. The choice one makes has life-changing consequences. There is no right answer; it's a crapshoot. Support groups for people with mental-health illnesses are one of the best resources to hear both pros and cons of talking to one's employer or remaining silent. Inevitably one will hear horror stories of those who remained silent and those who confided with their boss or with Human Resources about their disability. Many group members hold strong opinions. Emotions run high. One can leave a meeting more scared than when one arrived.

The responses from family and friends are no different. Some people with bipolar feel loved, supported and accepted. Others hear criticism and feel abandoned or rejected. Such responses are not necessarily without justification.

For Steven, the fear of discrimination determined his decision: to be silent. He wanted to receive promotions, to earn more income and to be recognized in the company and community as a successful man. He believed he could manage his disability. One reason for his confidence rested in the love and understanding Joan provided. She educated herself on the disorder, dropped into support groups when she needed help, accompanied Steven to most of his medical appointments and did all she could to maintain a calm and orderly home life. Much of Steven's success can be attributed to Joan's partnership in his vision for their life together.

Steven took responsibility for managing his disorder in the workplace, with attention to the smallest detail. He kept medication in his locked desk drawer, briefcase and car. He planned meetings for the morning, when he would be rested. Once a day he declared he needed exercise for "heart health." He would walk outside or, if the weather didn't cooperate, he would stroll the halls. When he had to fly to meetings, he took non-rush-hour flights. He always made sure he had sleeping medication with him because he knew lack of sleep was one of his major triggers. Calling Joan every day made the trips more successful and provided a "check-in" on his moods. On his return, Steven would work at home to organize the meeting's discussions and work on emails. His decision to participate with Dan in the "Spiritual Seekers" group provided him an important foundation. He needed God on his side.

Spiritual Reflection

Each week, the "Spiritual Seekers" spend a few minutes reconnecting and then members decide what they will read. Lately, they have been spending time on the book of Jeremiah. Tonight, they read from chapter 10 – silently, until a person finds a verse or phrase particularly relevant and shouts out, "Significance." Then that person explains the story behind the "significance."

On verse 14 Steven yells, "Significance." Everyone stops reading. Steven begins: "I have a personal story to tell and this Jeremiah verse will give you a clue as to moments when I become very angry." He reads the 14th verse: "Everyone is stupid and without knowledge." He introduces his explanation with an over-arching comment that many people judge others as stupid, especially in the political arena. Then he begins to share his judgments.

He explains to the group that he has diabetes, diagnosed when he was 10. He tells them the details of his "disease management" -- how and when he has to take medicine, how often and why he has to have his liver and kidneys tested, the schedule for visiting his doctors. He also describes attitudes people hold about diabetes. He then asks the question, "I bet you are wondering why I chose this verse. Well let me tell you the problem: Diabetes causes mood changes. Sugar levels vary and that causes mood changes. Mood changes cause problems in relationships. Problems in relationships cause stress. Stress messes with sugar levels."

He goes on to say that he manages his diabetes with precision because bruised relationships at work may result in poor personnel reviews. Many times, job insecurity, fear of job stagnation and reduced earnings result. These thoughts cause people to feel scared, frustrated, paranoid and angry. Co-workers then respond by rejecting the person and eventually the person will quit or get fired. The cause-and-effect model has now cemented into the work culture. But diabetes is just a chemical imbalance in the bloodstream. At times, he tells the group, he has gotten so angry and resentful from people's responses that he stares at each person saying, "It's a manageable disease" and says to himself, "You are all so stupid and ignorant." The group responds with supportive comments like, "How can people be so cruel?"

Of course, Steven is not talking about diabetes; he is talking about his bipolar illness. He believes that if he had said "bipolar," people not only would have responded differently to his story, but they would treat him differently in the future. He also is convinced someone would tell Dan, who was not at the meeting.

When Steven finishes his remarks, group members nod their heads and say, "Amen, Amen." And Steven thinks to himself, "If they only could know." Of course they can't because Steven has chosen to be silent . . . silent about a chronic illness that affects him every day. Only Joan can know.

Dan's Prayer

Thank you for guiding me through these many years working with Steven. He is like a brother. I am so grateful that years ago Joan secretly met me for lunch and explained Steven's life with bipolar disorder. You gave him many gifts. You opened my eyes so I could carve a place for him in the company, where his gifts could benefit so many people. I was one of them. Give him continued strength to manage his moods. Give him courage to tell his story as he remains active in the business community. He will then be an instrument of your grace and a voice for those living in silence. In Jesus' name, Amen.

Andrew

The Story

The youth group, called "Before and After" (for participants with curfews and those without), gathers in a mega-church to plan an urban immersion experience. The youth minister begins the meeting with a prayer. Andrew just wants to say, "Let's go!"

A young woman tapes paper to the walls and everyone begins offering ideas about activities. Andrew abruptly stands up, grabs a felt-tip marker, trots over to the paper and scribbles his ideas, narrating as he writes.

"Friday night let's go bowling on the north side, near where that teenager was killed last weekend, and eat at Matilda's. On Saturday morning we could volunteer at the crisis nursery center on 26th and Nicollet, and right before lunch -- who wants to feed those babies? -- we can join Habitat for Humanity and work on the house over in Brooklyn Park. We can grab some fast-food and then hightail it over to St. Stephen's Church for Loaves and Fishes. After clean-up, we can walk Franklin Avenue as a safety force. The girls can stop at establishments and place information on domestic violence in the women's bathrooms and you guys can place condoms in the men's bathrooms. We can return to the church and watch a killer movie, a funny movie and end up with a real scary thriller. I think I own all three. While watching movies we can play board games, too. I'll bring some from home. Sunday morning we can pick up some shut-in members of First Baptist Church in St. Paul and drop them off for a rare opportunity to worship. While we wait for the service to be over, we can pick up garbage in downtown St. Paul. Then run over to the church, pick up our passengers, return them to their homes and come back for a 'cook-your-favorite-recipe' lunch. We will be finished by 1:30, then go home. What a fun time and we'll be doing so much for the community!"

Andrew interrupts anyone who tries to speak and stares at people whose eyes are glazing over. He hands out maps, directions, schedules and an itemized budget. Deciding about carpooling ends the meeting. Most people leave amazed at Andrew's "take-charge" style and appreciative of a short meeting. A few feel resentful.

Immersion-weekend Friday comes and everybody dumps their gear at the church's front door and heads off to the youth room – everyone, that is, except Andrew. He is at home lying on his ripped-up couch, wrapped in torn blankets and watching old movies. He is consumed by feelings of guilt, shame, sadness and hopelessness. He has been on the couch for days. He's so very tired and doesn't even have the energy to brush his teeth or shower. His mind works slowly, as if each thought resists awareness. "Why am I like this?" he pleads to know. "God, why are you doing this to me?"

Comments on the Story

At the planning meeting, Andrew felt amazingly energized. Thoughts exploded in his brain like firecrackers and words spilled out of him like pebbles caught in an ocean wave. He's both blessed and cursed. Normally, adventure, tireless energy and creativity characterize him. People are drawn to his planning sessions just to watch him twirl; it is better than watching "I Love Lucy" reruns. At other times, Andrew's quick tongue and intense energy overwhelm his audience. He is easily angered. He is also unpredictable. He stays away from the group -- sometimes for several weeks. At those times he won't answer the phone even though it rests within reach.

A few years ago Andrew was referred to a psychiatrist, who diagnosed him with bipolar disorder. During the youth group's planning meeting, Andrew had held everyone's attention. His rapid thoughts, extreme high energy and grandiosity placed him in a state of hypomania. He may remain in this state for just a few hours or for several weeks. But another state -- depression -- is waiting to take control of his mind and compel him to live on the couch. This time he was depressed for more than a week. In a few days he became so worried that he might lose his job that he called his boss and told him that he had been in a car accident and could not work. On the fifth day, when he returned to his job, his production fell and his work was mediocre. He continued to worry about losing his job.

Andrew's family left him alone. They were tired of his selfish behavior. In the past he had taken medicine for his moods, but he had been feeling so good that two months ago he decided the pills were unnecessary. Andrew is in trouble.

Spiritual Reflection

The first two stories in the Bible tell of God's creation of humanity. These stories portray God as loving, steadfast and engaged. In the first story, God gathers dust, adds a little water and breathes life into it. With this breath, God creates men and women to be in the very "image" of God. Such intimacy reveals a God who blesses humanity and calls them "good." The second creation story helps us to wrap our arms around a God smitten with the needs of humanity but allowing people to make personal choices. God takes a rib from Adam and uses it to create a woman. God provides a garden, overflowing to meet the needs of these humans. This is the God that Andrew believes exists. He can imagine himself receiving the breath of God that has been passed down through all these generations. He knows in every cell of his being that God created people to love them in a powerful way. Yet when Andrew becomes depressed it is much more difficult to find this intimate God. Rather, his depression feels like punishment and then he gets confused. Right now, he feels abandoned by God. The feeling is so real that Andrew wonders if God even exists.

Trying to convince Andrew that his mental disorder fertilizes the soil for doubting God's love or even existence is nearly impossible when he is paralyzed by depression. When normalcy returns, Andrew celebrates a loving God creating people in God's own image. Maybe the next time he is depressed he can remember a spark of the divine and know that God will not leave him or forsake him, as recorded in the first few lines of Genesis. "So God created humankind in the divine image / In the image of God / humankind was created; / Male and female God created them."

Andrew's Prayer

Lord, I don't know what I'm doing. I wanted to go on that outing. I contributed so many ideas. I brought maps and stuff. Yet I feel so ashamed. I don't want to see any of those people again. I don't dislike them; I just feel the church would be better if I weren't around. I really like it when I have so much energy. Sometimes I know it's too much, though. Then sadness and a heavy feeling of worthlessness overcome me. I can't feel you or find you. I'm tired. Don't leave me again. You are my only hope. Amen.

Hope is the thing with feathers that perches in the soul -- and sings the tunes without the words -- and never stops at all. -- Emily Dickinson

For the bipolar community, hope has two very different dimensions. Hope can be the "feathers" -- heartfelt messages from friends and acquaintances to celebrate, recognize or lend support during life's ups and downs. This hope contributes to people feeling connected, valued and not ignored. In this context, hope offers good wishes, optimism and wishful thinking. Greeting cards, for example, allow one person to express a wish for another: I hope you have a wonderful day. I hope your birthday is the best yet. I hope you feel better soon. I hope you find peace in memories of your loved one. Such cards keep people connected to life's events. Not receiving cards can leave one feeling alone, invisible and sad. The hope of "feathers" is not to be discounted as frivolous or light-hearted. The power of kindness and wishes makes one's quality of life richer.

Hope has another dimension -- one that can change a person's belief in himself. Hope lives inside us as a vital reservoir of sustenance. It is omnipresent, a dependable ally. To understand this unconscious "sleeping giant" we need to experience how it works. Simply put, this dimension of hope opens up one's mind to visualize paths to stability: the crushing of chaos. For an individual with bipolar disorder, relief from pain and suffering means freedom to open windows to positive choices, self-advocacy and rest. To maintain this state, hope rises to the top, beckoning one to recognize this innate presence and cling to it. It empowers one to endure hardships and crawl inches to feet to gain a return to mood stability. This hope is tenacious.

Hope is just not the opposite of hopelessness. Much of the time, hope provides the impetus to do what needs to get done. Hopelessness places the person in a vice-grip with only quicksand for a foundation. There, shame thrives, imagination dims, energy sags and joy is a joke. This unimaginable cesspool of despair, experienced by people pierced by the demon bipolar depression, lends itself to suicidal ideation. Sometimes such obsessive thoughts of hopelessness felt time and time again convince a person to complete suicide. Such a decision leaves loved ones scarred for life. And the words of Rabbi Bebe of Nacham, an 18th century Classidic Master, ring with great wisdom: "To lose hope is to lose freedom, to lose oneself."

The dichotomy of hope vs. hopelessness is explored in some of this book's stories. For example, when the housing market collapses and Don imagines his family's financial ruin, he alienates friends and relatives along with his wife, Ji-Young. He spins out of control and loses all hope. Ji-Young fears for his safety and drives Don to the hospital. The story does not reveal if this is Don's first time without hope and he needs someone to hold onto hope for him, or if Don has been hospitalized before. But a reader can conclude that Ji-Young acts from hope that the hospitalization will return Don to a stable state of sanity. Additionally, Don will have created a list of actions he must take to maintain a dependable quality of life for himself and his family. Hope then becomes one aspect of action. Hope has the final say.

When one's life dips too far into depression, hope keeps a window open that allows us to hang on for another minute, hour or day until our hardships fade. In these devastating times, when shame, isolation and powerlessness consume a person with bipolar disorder and/or family and friends, hope frequently may feel like a fantasy or an undeserved gift only given to those seen as living a life of ease. In the midst of life's trials, hope does not shrink. Rather, it waits for the moment to be most valuable.

Because the term bipolar means two distinct mood elevations -- depression at one pole and hypomania (mania) on the opposite pole -- the perception of hope greatly differs. For the depressed person, hopelessness rules. She feels resentful toward anyone else with hope. However, mania or hypomania -- a lesser mood elevation -- also places hope at center stage. In this mood, hope becomes irrelevant. This is illustrated in George's story. George doesn't waste a minute of his time on such a useless concept as hope. He has all the answers. George believes only losers need the crutch of hope.

George already knows he has all the skills necessary to be successful as well as endless creative ideas than he can incorporate into his car construction. George is so confident in this project that he becomes furious with his wife, Helen, when she brings supper down to him. For George, eating or sleeping is just a waste of time. He is judgmental, cruel, happy, energized, creative and narcissistic. Helen, his only support person, cries alone, worries about her physical safety, rarely speaks to anyone about George's behaviors and constantly wishes for a life of ease and rest. She feels hopeless. Their bank account reinforces her belief that a real life is for those who do not live with a George.

Most family and friends of a person with bipolar disorder share some of the same miseries that nearly bury hope. These loving people have born the brunt of rage, blame, ugly words, threats and sleepless nights of terrifying worry. They know the patterns of their loved one. They hold memories of past experiences. Some behaviors could be called cruel, devastating and inexcusable. Wounds are deep. With the passage of time and with the heart remaining in love for the person with bipolar, the inevitable richness of hope takes hold and the relationship remains intact. But sometimes relationship work is too hard. With the memories of painful episodes, one believes these tough times will come again -- and again. He wrestles with the painful question that staying in the relationship will cost him a reliable sense of self and personal value. Hope has not evaporated. Sometimes it is hope that gives the individual the courage to leave the relationship. In like manner, for others hope is a guiding principle that keeps them close in mind, body, heart and soul.

To maintain a conscious decision to allow hope to do its job, people with bipolar and their support people can write an action plan. It is a useful document when symptomatic behaviors have escalated and the thought that "this is just a phase" is replaced with the conclusion that the suffering person needs a safe haven with greater professional help. At these very tense times, the person living on the couch watching TV for hours and not going to work, or the one not sleeping or eating because "life is all about me," will not agree to a trip to the psych unit. Many times the action plan focuses the support people to decisions and action. They need not fumble in confusion, insecurity and infighting. They get to the tasks at hand. Some situations require a call to the therapist. With greater concerns, a call to the psychiatrist's office becomes necessary.

And if the person expresses a major mood swing, like Don or George, the most compassionate decision is to get the person to the hospital.

It would be a disservice to support people to characterize them only in their role within the bipolar spectrum of issues. Support people have lives outside of the context of bipolar disorder. They have the issues of life. They pay taxes, have their own health problems, complain about their jobs, engage in other meaningful relationships and are invested in their own dreams for their lives. Nevertheless, they pay a price for their relationship with the individual with bipolar disorder. They may suffer from extreme loneliness because they feel the obligation not to talk about this high-maintenance person. To do so would be to violate the confidentiality inherent to this primary relationship. The result is they suffer alone, mirroring the life of the person with bipolar. If hope has its way, the support person will establish his own friends, interests and activities. And he will spend time with professional people for help in traversing relationship boundaries and processing the hard times and those in between.

The characterization of hope as actions to reach goals or of sustaining a person during profound suffering may be difficult to grasp. Two examples of hope's persistence may give more clarity. One example is humorous, the other life-sustaining for people fearing for the life of a child.

In 1951, Charles Schulz created the comic strip Peanuts, which ran for nearly fifty years. The main character, Charlie Brown, was shy and easily manipulated by the dozen or more characters, yet he continued to live in hope for a better life. One of the more popular protagonists was Lucy, a loudmouth neighbor who repeatedly reduced Charlie Brown to shameful experiences.

A regular story line placed Lucy as the holder for Charlie Brown's efforts to kick a football. Each time he believed that Lucy would hold the ball. Each time she pulled it away at the last moment and Charlie Brown would back-flip onto the ground. Lucy then would make some mean remark that left Charlie Brown walking off the field with his head hung low. Charlie Brown clung to hope each time he asked Lucy to hold the ball. Lucy saw hope as a weakness and used this perception to humiliate Charlie Brown over years of comic strips and TV specials. Yet time and again Charlie Brown was convinced that Lucy would hold the ball and he would be able to kick it. It never happened. Lucy never gave Charlie his joy.

Giving up one's goal leaves just one option: hopelessness. This is as true for organizations as it is for individuals. National organizations understand the power and energy of sustained hope. They magnify hope and minimize hopelessness. They demand hope in action to uplift those in extreme suffering to resist the urge to drop into the dark well of hopelessness. They put hope to work.

An example of a national organization using hope as an essential element of positive action is the AMBER Alert. This nationwide child abduction alert system dates to 1996 and was created after nine-year-old Amber Hagerman was abducted and murdered in Texas. Since then, the alert has saved countless children's lives around the country. Hope here is not wishful thinking that a child will be found before a tragedy occurs. Rather, hope persists because an AMBER Alert brings together law enforcement, family and friends, the general public and neighbors to find the child. For months, multiple leads by strangers are given to the police, any person even remotely connected to the child gets interviewed, and evidence is examined and labeled. Those efforts offer hope to these terrified families. No parent or family is left alone to work with just their local police. Hope is operating in people as they offer their services to bring together an army of professionals and dedicated volunteers to locate the child alive.

In 1984 the National Center for Missing and Exploited Children became the umbrella organization for AMBER Alert and other efforts to rescue children from predators. Hope is alive in each action. Indeed, at one point the organization used the tagline "30 years of Hope." More specifically the tag line could read, "With hope, 30 years of love."

Known or unknown, too many people with bipolar disorder may dismiss or diminish the hope that enables them to self-care or advocate for themselves. Their attitudes are challenged or minimized when they listen to others who walk the same path as they do. Hearts beat with hope when public figures discloses that they live with bipolar disorder and elaborate on the effects bipolar has had on their personal lives or careers. A connection is felt when these people share that they have self-medicated in dangerous ways, have denied their diagnosis, and/or stopped taking medications. When they elaborate on the consequences of these destructive decisions, as well as their daily routines to maximize mood stability, hope rises up for the listener with the power of an awesome ocean wave. When they share that for months or years they have lived without mood swings with the help of personal and professional skills, compassion and reliability, hope also swells. Hearing these stories, people with the disorder and support people can believe with greater confidence that bipolar does not need to be the controlling enemy in their lives. The twins of stigma and shame need not have the power society has given them

When people with bipolar disorder look at their family of origin and extended family, they may see relatives who suffered all their lives from the lack of professional help. They also may know a relative with bipolar who tried several approaches to managing the disorder and lived long periods of time "in ease." Thus there is hope when a family member is known to work hard to salvage the quality of her life. Such a scenario affords those who follow to copy her strategy; hope is passed on from one family member to another. Likewise, suffering people can hear success stories in their support groups and hold tighter to hope. And friends can be an outlet that helps a person remain hopeful.

All the positive decisions and actions, along with a vision of the future, are fed by the relationship one has with hope. Hope is helpful as a server of wishful thinking and optimism. Hope offers ways for someone to enhance his life and provides the strength to make it through another day. Hope never leaves; it just keeps helping each person not to lose his soul.

My Story

The conscious recognition that hope delivers a strong potion of survival when one is under distress came to me in college. Living in the dorm at times mirrored a therapy group without a therapist or time limitation. At spontaneous gatherings, we laughed until tears streaked our faces, cried until silence filled the room, and processed our families of origin until we knew no more wisdom. Each person left the group with three engraved stones: Love -- no one lives alone here. Hope -- no one needs to figure out fears alone. Faith -- the power of the group exceeds anyone's ego. I vividly remember conversations about hope and hopelessness. I applauded hope. It visited me when despair was slapping me around. Hope insisted I look back to early childhood in order to endure current misery.

When I was a tyke, my family lived in the shame of Dad being the town drunk, of bill collectors knocking at our door and of social services concluding that the kids would be better off in foster families. To deal with these oppressive burdens, my mother farmed my three older siblings to relatives and me to neighbors over sixty years old. "Mrs. Kindness" lovingly cared for my basic needs and added fresh-baked bread with jam from the fruit of backyard bushes. When my belly hurt she toasted bread, soaked it in warm milk and sprinkled it with sugar. She loved me with tender care and a sweet heart. Her husband was a tough old goat, "Mr. Ugly" until he took over my daytime care. A lumberjack by trade, he probably fit the stereotypical lifestyle of those guys. Wake up to the repeated yell from the cook, "Daylight in the swamp"; eat before dawn; saw wood until near dark. According to lumberjack history, the men were tight fisted, foul-mouthed drunkards who lived off small-town businesses, including "ladies of the night."

When the forests were stripped, "Mr. Ugly" returned to his small rural town, married and fathered a son. His wife showed the visible signs of a battered woman and his son was treated in much the same manner. With my arrival, "Mr. Ugly" transformed into "Mr. Kindness." No one understood this miraculous change. All I know is that every day he showered me with unconditional love. He fostered in me the belief that trust is true, holding hands walking down the street means love, and cemeteries can be the best playground. This solid foundation of self-esteem placed a voice of hope in my brain: Hope is real. Hope is remembered. Hope leads to healing.

When sexual assaults and months of depressions separated my body from my mind, heart and soul, I chose the healing path of professional therapy. When alcohol and drugs were the accepted self-medicating decisions of people around me, I held firmly against such strategies. Alcohol terrified me; what a gift from hope's power. When bipolar disorder came to claim my sanity and life, I eventually grabbed on to the wings of hope. It tossed me at the doorstep of a different therapist -- a dear friend of many years. During a sweet "check-up" dinner, I abruptly turned the agenda to my life story. She knew I was in deep trouble.

My friend worked at a mental-health/chemical-dependency clinic. She slipped into the conversation that I should talk to the psychiatrist at the clinic, her trusted colleague. "OK; what the heck," I responded. In five days I was in his office. Two hours later, I heard the diagnosis: bipolar disorder. I remember thinking I must have a real problem, not just a stress reaction to my demanding life.

The doctor prescribed lithium and my life changed. Within several days I lived in less inner chaos. Rooms had 90 degree corners, the cement under my feet held me without slippage. My car had identifiable gas and brake pedals, and the steering wheel moved the car exactly as I had turned it. These changes sounded strange to people, even to me. Yet, the feeling of some level of control began seeping into my mind. Hope seemed one step ahead of me and available to me without my request. When I sank into places where hope seemed to be a thing of the past, I nevertheless scraped along, healing two steps forward, one step back.

It was not my multiple educational degrees that motivated me to heal. It was not luck that resources for healing came my way. It was not a loving God fixing me. It was not traveling in many parts of the world that gave me my self-medication. It was not friends whose pain equaled or was greater than mine that offered me wisdom to learn healing ways. Rather, it was the presence of hope, never named but always understood, that led me to use all my energy to heal.

I believe the only times when hope was not a dependable force in my life were when I lived in periods of hypomania. In that mood, I became greater than hope. Hope was frail and weak; I was strong and sturdy. When such a fun and rewarding mood as mania-hypomania ended, as it always does, hope took the oars of my canoe and brought me safely to the shores of mood management. Even today, with more than twenty-five years of experiencing changes in my moods and ignoring several signs of danger, hope paddles me back to a past life of transformations. The memories of "Mr. and Mrs. Kindness" nearly bring the phone to my hand to make the call to schedule a doctor's appointment.

Hope -- whether acknowledged or not -- lives inside everyone. Hope and healing with bipolar come with some well-tried tools, and spirit ties it all together to claim wholeness and abundance for all people.

Healing

Emily

The Story

At 41, Emily feels her life is finally coming together. Six years have passed since her "jail time" in the psych unit. Today, sitting on the deck of her condo, waiting for an e-mail confirming her job promotion, she marvels at the fact she survived the tumultuous years preceding her hospitalization. Now it is just consistent work to maintain her present stability. Not every day is easy, but she has committed herself to regularly keeping a check on her moods and recording troubling events about which she will speak to her psychiatrist on her next visit. She has established friends and colleagues who she has entrusted with giving her feedback when she exhibits symptoms that may indicate a repeat of past bipolar symptoms. Not often does Emily sit with her memories of long ago. But today is a new job, a new day, so thoughts of yesterdays surface. They come easily to her mind.

Emily labels her life as one big diagnostic runaround. In third grade she was tested for learning disabilities. The results showed a significant reading problem. Her parents worked with the school and hired private tutors. In fifth grade, teachers complained that she disturbed the classroom dynamics with her constant chatting, squirming and joking. Frustrated with Emily's problems, her parents really wanted to tell Emily to just listen to the teacher and stop causing problems. Instead, they called Emily's pediatrician. The doctor listened to the concerns of Emily's parents and sat down for a conversation with Emily. He concluded that she should be tested for Attention Deficit Hyperactivity Disorder (ADHD). A blind test with Emily's teachers was administered, followed by an additional computerized test. The results left no room for doubt. Emily needed medication and close monitoring to treat her ADHD. Once that happened, her schoolwork improved, but Emily became aware of another feeling -- anxiety.

In high school, Emily joined every club possible and held leadership positions in many of them. At the same time, she shed friends and wandered home alone after school activities. Eventually a teacher noticed the dichotomy between Emily's extra-curricular activities and the look of an unhappy teenager. The teacher spoke with the guidance counselor, who decided to recommend to Emily's folks that she undergo psychological testing. The parents agreed. Emily was 17. The results showed that she ranked high on the anxiety measurements. Counseling was recommended, so every week Emily took a bus to Lutheran Social Services to meet with a therapist. From Emily's perspective, however, therapy wasted her time.

In college, Emily's anxiety worsened and depression entered her life. Her stomach began to ache and at times she felt significant pain. After a few trips to the infirmary, the doctor suggested she see a psychiatrist. She did. He listened for a few weeks and then told her to "find a boyfriend, date for awhile and then have another woman steal him away." Emily felt shamed and inadequate. Neither her depressions nor her anxiety lessened.

Emily married at 24. She believed a loving and secure marriage would protect her from her lifelong misery. For several years her belief held true. She received a promotion to marketing in a medical technology company. Bob, her husband, worked long hours as a salesman. He wrote strategic plans, dined with clients and travelled to locations for consultations. Work occupied their lives.

Both Emily and Bob engaged in community activities. Bob raised money for the United Way and particularly enjoyed his membership on the local orchestra's board of directors. Emily enjoyed Rotary luncheons and League of Women Voters activities. In the League, she served with recognition on several committees and with consistent pressure accepted the role of president. Emily believed that even with added responsibilities she could manage her mental-health illness.

Bob and Emily had established a circle of married friends that met for dinner when one of them had a birthday. Conversations included life with children. Most of the stories revolved around soccer, hockey, tennis, swimming and debate competitions. Bob and Emily had talked about having children, and in six years Jason and Molly were born. Emily quit her job to be a full-time parent. Bob and Emily were happy and children's activities took most of their time. Emily volunteered at Molly's pre-school as well as in Jason's third-grade class. The teachers loved her and the kids enjoyed her playfulness.

Emily's ADHD worked well in the school setting. Her anxiety proved useful when chairing meetings; they always finished in record time. No one complained. She believed her medications would hide any concrete signs of instability. Bob, however, noticed changes in her. He worried that her medications might need to be changed or that she had stopped taking some of them. He was concerned that she was headed for a deep depression or the hurtful wit from intense anxiety. Eventually her moods did change. Both Bob and the kids became victims of Emily's criticisms, anger, demands and rejections.

One evening at dinner Jason was silent and withdrawn. At bedtime Bob went to read Jason his "good-night" book and asked him about his dinnertime behavior. Jason looked scared. With Bob's prodding Jason said, "A few nights ago Mom locked herself in her bedroom and when Molly and I told her we were hungry, she told us to go away." He sobbed and told his Dad, "I don't think Mom loves me anymore."

Bob needed to hear no more. He needed to protect his children. Emily had scarred the family. Bob would not tolerate this betrayal. The next day Bob told Emily he wanted a divorce. He was finished. Hope had dried up. He took the kids to a hotel, phoned a mediation service and made an appointment. Bob arrived for the meeting; Emily did not. That was the end of mediation.

Emily had conceived of a plan to end her life of chaos without the children ever knowing her death was intentional. It took her a few weeks to work out every detail and wait for the perfect rainstorm. When that day came, Emily drove her car onto the mountainous road she typically travelled to visit her first college roommate. The road looked like a sheet of ice. The radio blasted Janis Joplin's "Me and Bobby McGee." Approaching the sharp turn she had expected, she did not move the steering wheel. Her car rolled several times and with dust and debris flying everywhere, it landed upside down in a ravine.

Even with reduced visibility, a trucker noticed the broken railing and assumed that someone had ripped through the protective chain. He looked down the steep hill and noticed the upturned dirt, branches and small trees. The rain reflected on a car's mirror. He pulled his rig up until it nearly touched the chain. Then he called 911 and ran down the hill to check for life. Emily, trapped from bent metal, still breathed. Officers arrived, called for an ambulance and whispered to the trucker, "It's a miracle she's alive."

After days in intensive care, Emily was moved to the psychiatric unit in the hospital. A doctor met with her and took individual and family histories. Except for Emily's reading disability, the psychiatrist determined that she has bipolar disorder. The psychiatrist prescribed lithium. In about ten days, Emily felt a flicker of hope.

Comments on the Story

Emily's story of repeated tests, diagnoses and medication trials left her feeling worthless and unimportant. No pill eliminates the symptoms of bipolar disorder, anxiety, learning disabilities or Attention Deficit Hyperactivity Disorder. No cure exists. But the best advice most psychiatrists give their patients is to take prescribed medicine, enter talk or cognitive therapy, establish support systems and show up for doctor's appointments with questions and reports of medication side-effects, unusual behaviors, stressors and general quality of life.

It is a challenge for a doctor to plow through records from various sources, including the patient, to establish a treatment protocol. Most likely, the psychiatrist will prescribe medication for the symptoms that most reduce the quality of a patient's life. Typically, bipolar disorder will receive the first attention. When moods stabilize, attention then will be given to any remaining problems that have been identified.

Spiritual Reflection

In the midst of mood swings, some people may find it difficult to believe that a loving God exists, or maybe the thought crosses their mind that a loving God exists, but not for them. The Bible says differently.

God established a nation from nomads and nobodies to call people to a better life, a sustainable world and a steadfast relationship. When the folks strayed from promises of life that God had freely given, God sent messengers -- prophets -- to redirect these chosen people to a life of blessings.

It would be foolish to suggest that God promised a perfect life or that each person would be protected from harm or illness or pain. But scripture does record God's interventions that provided people both nurturance and substance. During the Exodus, the people of God -- roaming in the desert for four decades -- became angry for lack of food. God provided water, manna and quail. When Hagar, a mother of a young son, placed her child under a bush so she did not have to watch him die, God heard the voice of her baby. An angel spoke to Hagar: "Lift up the boy. . . . I will make a great nation of him."

Scripture records Jesus touching the disenfranchised, healing the sick, teaching of God's presence and offering the words, "Come to me, all you who are weary and burdened, and I will give you rest. Take my yoke upon you and learn from me, for I am gentle and humble in heart, and you will find rest for your souls. For my yoke is easy and my burden is light."

Some people believe that with consistent prayer, God will always provide relief. Scripture also records people praying for help and receiving none. Prayer doesn't mean God waits around to grant only certain people their requests. Rather, prayer is a conversation with God that provides a relationship instead of abandonment; an opportunity to express gratitude instead of hostility and petitions instead of demands. Like any other relationship, each person must show up. Emily finally did.

Emily's prayer

You, who have remained in my heart and have walked with me through a forest of my paths, continue to bathe me in your mercy. You call us to love ourselves. Remove any barrier to my acceptance of my disorder and thus provide the love I have most difficulty giving myself. Continue guiding me to your vision for my life. Amen.

JOSEPH

The Story

Joseph cannot envision any future better than today. It's his 23rd birthday and he is turning in his last nerve-wracking paper of the semester. He hopes he doesn't see his professor. "What a joke. I could have taught that class so much better," Joseph tells himself. Now, however, that doesn't matter because Joseph likes parties and his party tonight will rock.

With nothing holding him back, he plans every detail of his celebration. He stops at the liquor store and buys eight six-packs of different beers. Everyone must be happy. The grocery store is next for burgers, steaks and vegetables for the grill, along with three different pies -- even though he knows someone will bring a funny personalized cake. With drinks and food, he drives home thinking about his disorganized and messy house. It's a "guy thing," he decides. He doesn't connect the chaos in his life with his decision a while back to stop taking his mood-disorder medication.

Once home, he shoves stuff around to make space for his packages. He then decides to call his love interest, Molly, to come over and help him prepare for the party. "Sure," she responds, "as soon as I walk the dogs and stop by Dad's condo." Joseph is miffed. Even though they met just a few weeks ago, he is ready to be "exclusive" and hopes she is, too.

He turns on his iPod and, with music blaring, he begins to plow through the disorganization. He cleans with a rare vigor. In four hours his friends will arrive. He secretly envisions them bringing just the right gifts, not cleaning supplies like last year. After an hour or so, he realizes his place is still such a mess. He berates himself. He calls himself a failure. He knows no one really wants to come to his stupid party. He just wants to lie down. Joseph no longer cares that his refrigerator has moldy food or that his bathroom stinks. He feels sad about everything. His negative self-talk repeats and repeats in his brain. So many regrets come to mind. One is the paper he turned in today. What a disgrace. He never wants to see his professor again. The doorbell chimes. Molly waits, then she calls him. Joseph does not go to the door and he does not answer his cell phone. His party is over before it begins.

Comments on the Story

Joseph knows his moods can change daily or even more than once in a day. On a sunny morning he can feel the warmth on his back, hear a chirping bird and enjoy laughter coming from a couple nearby. His fellow students laugh at his jokes and tell him their day is brighter because of his unique personality. Other times, he hides. He feels despair. Not too long ago a classmate told him, "Joseph, when you come to class, I just don't know who I will see."

Many people with bipolar disorder who regularly take their medications feel so healthy and strong that they stop. After all, it is sick people who take pills, not those who already feel fine. This logic undermines a consistent regimen of mood management. Eventually, the person returns to mood swings and calls his doctor, sometimes waiting several weeks before an appointment is available.

Besides the challenges of a person with bipolar regularly taking his meds, other problems exist for both doctor and patient. Diagnosing this disorder from other behavior patterns requires a doctor to take a thorough family history, inquire about the specific presenting problems, and differentiate between other similar symptoms, such as Attention Deficit Hyperactivity Disorder, depression with anxiety, or good and bad feelings related to alcohol or drug use. If medication is appropriate, trials will begin. Weeks may pass before one's medications bring the desirable results. Many people with bipolar take several medications, including some to address side effects of the primary medication.

Like Joseph, whose bipolar symptoms may erupt daily or every few days, the possibility of self-confidence, creative impulses or a heightened sense of self-esteem can occur. So can self-loathing, despair and hopelessness.

Each mood swing cannot be controlled by just waiting it out or thinking more rationally. Rather, each pole feels like life's reality, not a periodic state of mind.

Relationships suffer because of these unpredictable and frequent mood changes. Molly sees in Joseph a good heart. She tells him he is a good person. Sometimes he believes her. Other times he feels unworthy of her attention and care. Molly doesn't know which Joseph to believe.

Spiritual Reflection

Molly prays for healing within Joseph. Her hope lives in the stories she has learned in her Bible study of Jesus' ministry. She has talked to Joseph about his religious beliefs, but he shrugs off the topic. "My grandfather was a minister, my Dad a deacon. I have had enough of church," he says. These words hurt her because her faith brings her joy, strength and peace. She knows his attitude will be a deal breaker in their relationship.

She invites Joseph to attend her Bible study but he dismisses the idea. So she suggests a less threatening offer -- go to church and listen to a lecture/discussion of the similarities among Judaism, Islam and Christianity. He finds the idea intriguing but at the last moment bows out. Molly tells Joseph that her deepening faith gives her a joy she has never felt before. He smirks. He surely has never felt the "joy."

Joseph's heart has hardened to church and to the Bible verses memorized so long ago. He calls himself a spiritual person, not a religious one. He would rather walk in the woods with Molly, spread a blanket on the grass and speak words of endearment. But Joseph doesn't ask Molly for such a stroll. His heart aches for secure, trusting and safe relationships but he readily admits he's the first to drop a friend. Sometimes his anger gets the best of him. Other times he simply doesn't show up for a "hang out." Love slips through his fingers; so does God.

Joseph's Prayer

You are as dependable as I am. Really, no matter how I talk to Molly about "joy," I do believe you exist. You are so close when my world spins in a pleasurable orbit. But when negative feelings erupt inside of me, you are gone. Nothing that I once learned or believed today makes any sense. Then I get so angry that you won't touch me;

that you have abandoned me. I want to make my relationship with Molly grow. She wants you to be part of the equation. Okay. I just need to know you will always be there. Amen.

BEATRICE & HAROLD

The story

I hurt. My muscles feel torn, my bones raw from grinding one joint onto another. Feeding, bathing and changing diapers at the so-called "Hope Village" nursing home wears on me. I give and give -- never enough. No one notices me. Just like at home. Harold lies on the couch with that crusty, dirty towel covering his sagging body and the smelly, brown-stained pillow smashed under his head. He watches television all day. When I get home from work, I enter the house and shout, "I'm home." But he doesn't bother to even respond.

Harold has been on that couch for days. He never washes; his oily hair sticks to his head. He never helps me. He doesn't talk to me or answer the phone. He drags me down. My sister tells me I should divorce him. But my job provides us with insurance. Besides, I can't hire an attorney. I can't even stop at McDonald's. One flower in my week is church. I have friends there. My pastor of several years, patting my chapped and swollen fingers, tells me that none of us is given more than we can handle and I should pray for Harold. I feel guilty.

I do remember, though, that years ago Harold rode a high wave. For our tenth wedding anniversary, we celebrated all year long. We went dancing, had neighbors over for dinner and joined a bowling league. I slid into the car and Harold announced that we should travel, see the world. The sky's the limit, he said. We would go first-class; see places others only imagined. We would wear designer clothes and bring home gifts for everyone. He called dozens of travel agencies. He had so many ideas I couldn't keep track of them. He would wake me in the middle of the night with a dazzling new one. I reminded him we didn't have the money for all his ideas, but he just retorted that I deserved the best. He would whip out one map after another, creating stories of ports and places we must go. Night and day he worked on our adventure. He seemed so happy and animated. One day, the credit-card bill came. He had purchased first-class airline tickets, pre-paid cruises, guided tours and I don't even remember what else. He had spent thousands and thousands of dollars. Today, seven years later, I still make credit-card payments. We will never be free. Harold hasn't been the same since. I loved him once. Now I just take care of him. And like everyone else, he never says thank you.

Comments on the Story

Harold spent many years functioning adequately in his life and relationships. He held several jobs; each paid the bills. He did not want his wife to work or drive. Whatever triggered his first mania episode remains a mystery. His family's history is known only through stories. He knew his mother went to stay with an aunt for a while because of some unknown ailment. Harold's brother takes sleeping pills. Not much more is known.

When Harold decided on his special anniversary gift for his beloved wife, he began searching for ideal vacation spots. His focus, concentration and energy consumed him. His job suffered but he kept that information private. In just over three months he lost his job, spent all the savings, maxed out his two credit cards, gained new friends and then lost them all. His worry over his and Beatrice's financial situation landed him in a constant state of depression, anger and sleepless nights.

Harold has no desire to cause catastrophic problems and destroy his marriage. He just doesn't tell Beatrice his thoughts. Family and friends stay away. Beatrice only has her sister and her church as escape valves. Her sister nags her, "Divorce the loser." Beatrice knows she can't stretch her dollars to live alone, and her wedding vows guide her decisions: ". . . in sickness and in health. . . ."

Harold's depression will lift; he may or may not totally regain vitality. He may never have another mania episode or clinical depression. If he would see a doctor, a family history would be recorded, a diagnosis determined and medications prescribed. With correct medical management, education and support for both Harold and Beatrice, their quality of life could be restored. They don't take the risk.

Spiritual Reflection

When one experiences persistent physical sickness, the question often arises from the suffering person or from his support person, "Where is God?" This question is legitimate. After all, if God is all-powerful, why do people suffer? At least minimally, "Why do the innocent suffer?" More specifically, "Why do my children suffer?" These questions deserve to be asked directly of God. They have been.

In the Bible, the story of Job -- written more than 2,000 years ago -- gets to the heart of these legitimate questions. Job had everything: loving family, wealth, respect in his community and love of God. His situation drastically changed through the intervention of Satan. Job became dreadfully sick. His body oozed from boils, sores and scabs. He stunk. No physician or medicine could cure him. He wanted to die. From his unbearable pain, he cried out to God, "Why give light to those in misery? Why give life to embittered souls?" These cries have been uttered by many people with bipolar disorder and by their supporters. In anguish, some scream out to God the bitter questions: "Why me?" or "When will you lift this pain?"

Support people are often scared, confused and angry, and have similar questions for God: "How can the child I bore live with so much pain?" "Can I continue to be supportive?" "Is it best for me to back off." Sometimes, with the best intention, the support person asks the person with bipolar or God, "What did I do that I must deal with this on-going mess?"

Friends visit Job. Upon seeing his extreme suffering, the friends sit with him in silence for seven days. Finally, Job speaks: "Why didn't I die at birth? . . . I have no peace; I have no quiet; I have no rest -- only turmoil." One of his friends responds that Job brought this suffering on himself. The friend recommends he plead to God for restoration of his health because God is great and good. He concludes that Job just needs to be patient.

Job can't get there. Disappointed in his friend's advice, Job knows this person really does not understand his despair and physical pain. Job spits out that he is "past hope." He will cry to God out of his "anguish in his heart" and the "bitterness in his soul."

After Job's agonizing physical pain, blaming of friends and cries to die, God appears to him and his friends. Now the question of why the innocent should suffer must be answered by God. Instead, in this story, God turns the tables and asks Job and his friends a series of questions -- four chapters / 129 verses long.

The storytellers use the tale of Job not to answer the question of why the innocent suffer. Rather, each generation, community and family must wrestle with this desperate and all-consuming question. The story of Job only gives one message: God does not cause the suffering or death of people. God does not determine who should suffer or die and who should not. Humanity is left with the question.

Harold's Prayer

Lord, I cry to you from this sunken couch. The light hurts my eyes. I pull the shades. I don't understand this suffering. What did I do to deserve this? Only bills from long ago remind me I once had good times. Problems occupy me. I am overwhelmed. My wife provides me food, not nourishment. No one comes just to sit with me. I am so alone, so fat. I exist in despair and hopelessness. Grant me relief -- whatever form that may take. Amen.

Hank & Stone

The Story

When I am in the woods training my Lab, Stone, for duck hunting, I hear myself singing to the great Creator that hymn I learned as a kid:

> I've got the joy, joy, joy, joy
> Down in my heart,
> Where?
> Down in my heart
> Where?
> Down in my heart
> I've got the joy, joy, joy, joy
> Down in my heart
> Where?
> Down in my heart to stay
> The devil he won't find me 'cause its
> Down in my heart
> Where?
> Down in my heart
> Where?
> Down in my heart
> The devil he won't find me 'cause its
> Down in my heart
> Where?
> Down in my heart to stay.

Stone doesn't like my singing. He just stares at me. Funny dog. We've been through a lot together. Except for a few of my outings at the "nut" ward" -- never during hunting season -- Stone has been my buddy.

I married my high school sweetheart and we had three kids. Miracle upon miracle, after seventeen years of estrangement, my boys and I are getting along. Around the fire at night, after the women and grandkids have gone to bed, the boys and me sit with a couple of beers. I have shared some of my life and they have shared some of the fear, anger, hurt and judgments they felt during bad family times.

One day when they were little, I blew my stack. I screamed at my wife with words I'd rather not have in my brain. I slammed the door on my way out and never looked back. I'm real sorry about that. I just couldn't help it. Stone never had any trouble with me. Of course, there was that one time when I couldn't even crawl to the front door to let him out. He found a proper place and after doing his business, he just crawled back on the couch. It belongs to both of us.

Next time the boys come I gotta talk to them about my Mom and my brothers, who also have my brain disease. They must learn how to take care of each other and my grandkids and learn how I found God up here in "God's Country."

My spirit roams the marshes and meadows here where God lives with me and me with Him. I used to go to church. In fact I rather liked it, even sang in the choir. Then I flew off the handle and got stuck in the "nut ward." I really needed someone to take care of Stone. But no one volunteered. Never felt so alone.

Stone's now thirteen. He has helped me to stand upright. And somehow when I get a bit whacky he just sits me down for a while and then we take the canoe up Little Brook Creek and soon I'm okay again.

I believe God sent me old Stone. And the Lord better be prepared to hold my heart when Stone goes. I'll need more than a duck season to get my feet steady on the ground. In fact, God better never take Stone during duck season. I might not make it through that double banger.

The next thing God's gotta do is send me a new Stone -- not a replacement, just a good retrievin' one for ducks and my "spirit." I know when God sends that dog, the angels of duck hunters will be a clappin' and I'll have to start all over again with treats, whistles and pats on the dog's head.

God keeps an eye on me and Stone. And when I go into town and pass that little brick church, I always make the sign of the cross, tip my hat and say, "Thank you Lord." I know I don't need to do that. God's got his ducks in a row.

Story Comments
Some families have multiple members diagnosed with bipolar disorder, depression or substance abuse. In Hank's family of origin, three of four living members have some mental-health disease. Hank's dad, John, does not.

From the time he was a child, Hank helped his dad with chores at home and at the community center for their town of 4,500 people. Hank got good grades all through school. He had no idea that bipolar disorder was going to wreck his life. At twenty-three he married his high school sweetheart. They had three sons. Hank was forty-two when his wife died suddenly, leaving him to raise the boys. Hank never climbed out of that dark hole until anger seemed to control his whole life. He went between sorrow and rage. The boys experienced the worst of his mean behaviors. John ran out of ideas about how to help his son. After months of Hank's extreme moods, John called Doc Dahlstrom. And then John drove Hank the sixty miles to the closest hospital.

Hank did well in treatment. He visited a grief counselor twice a week. The hospital psychiatrist talked at length with Hank and recorded a complete family history. With this information and with a conversation with John about Hank's moods, the doctor diagnosed Hank with bipolar disorder. He placed him on Lamictal, a medication that stabilized Hank's moods.

Toward the end of treatment, Hank got a day pass. He bought a used fishing rod and went to a nearby lake. Feelings of serenity filled him. Anticipation of the next step in his life occupied his mind as he fished. Hank knew that to keep himself healthy he needed a strict medical regimen, a trusted pharmacy, Dr. Dalhstrom and his dad. He also knew he needed the Creator God he could talk to while fishing or hunting from his beat-up boat.

On the way home from the hospital, Hank and his dad stopped at a café for a good meal. There Hank saw a bulletin board with a for-sale notice about a funny looking Labrador named Ruffy. Hank thought, "I just found me the last piece of my new peaceful life at the old family cabin up north. God, medicine, earth, moon and this dog who definitely needs a new name."

Hank is now doing well because of his father's kindness and compassion toward him and the boys. John's experiences with other family members prepared him for helping Hank. As John supports each family member, he also needs recognition and sometimes relief from his caregiving. He is fortunate. He lives in a town where he doesn't lock his car or his house. Neighbors and friends help him with their "let's sit down and have a cup of coffee" time. They work together on house repairs and sometimes they go hunting with Hank.

Another resource is Florence Johnson, whose son has gone out of town twice for chemical-dependency treatment. Every other month, John and Florence join a small group of people for coffee. They talk, laugh and listen. Their secret motto is, "Misery loves miserable people." They use that saying to remind themselves that by sticking together, misery moves someplace else.

Spiritual Reflection

People come to God, or their Higher Power, or Creator God or Divine spirit from many roads. Each path needs to be respected. Sometimes when people with bipolar disorder feel particularly wrapped in grandiosity and unleashed energy to express that mood of elevated self-esteem, they may reach out to God, run in nature's rich paths or swim for an hour at the health club. When living in stability, they may slow down to do the same activities as others around them. Some may meditate, chant or read their Bible. We come to the Holy with what we have when we have it.

Hank loved God. Hank never blamed God for his bipolar disorder, nor did he feel abandoned. Maybe living out in the boat and marshes with fishing rods and rifles gave Hank a feeling that God lived dangerously too -- right inside Hank's heart.

The Israelites in the Genesis creation stories came to God confused, frightened, worried and vulnerable. They knew they had disobeyed God. They heard about God's faithfulness and granting free choice.

Generations later the Israelites came to God confused, frightened, worried and vulnerable again. They heard a joy-filled story telling them that God created every molecule in the universe and lifted up humanity to be created in God's own image and to have stewardship of all that God had created. Hank loved these stories. The imagery of a lush garden, of the first moon and of God breathing into him the breath of life calmed him to feel a deep connection to God.

God waits. God is patient. Many people have found a way to pray and meditate and feel God's presence. With such comfort, they have a feeling of well-being that their life matters to themselves and God. Whenever people hurt, God is present. Whenever people are angry, God is loving enough to hear all the words. For those who have wrestled with God well into the night, God remains steadfast.

People throughout the centuries have asked questions about the nature of God. Maybe all we need to know is that God welcomes all people and will be a constant presence with them whatever their circumstances -- even people with bipolar disorder whose faith comes and goes.

Hank's Prayer

Thank you Lord God for the ducks, the sunrise and the moon to light my way in the dark. Thank you for your presence in every moment of my life. Bless my family and keep Stone smiling every time I say, "Let's take a walk, boy." Amen.

Kisha

The Story

Kisha structures her life around her new job as a computer wizard, her new boyfriend, her Mom and her dog, Jingles.

The man in her life, Sam, a veterinarian, makes her laugh and they see each other almost every day, except when she goes home to her family of origin. Sam went to meet her mother and brother James -- once. Their snappy comments, negative references to other extended family members and bad food made Sam so uncomfortable that he told Kisha he would rather stay away. Kisha's younger brother, Franklin, stays away too. Kisha meets him for coffee, but talking about the family brings up so many painful memories that they focus on each others' friends and church.

James provides the most angst. He simply flies high. He calls night and day with goofy ideas. Kisha believes if he would spend more time on the problems he creates, the family would be happier. James married at 21, divorced at 26, and is the father of one child, Dorinda. James rarely sees his daughter. He would rather drink with the boys and kiss the ladies. Three weeks ago, James had trouble with his computer and asked Kisha to fix it. She went to his totally disorganized apartment. There on his computer she found many pornography websites; she deleted them and told her brother to never again ask her for help.

Kisha regularly attends her Baptist church. She finds strength and solace there. She knows missing church makes her week more difficult. Every Sunday, Kisha drives to her Mom's home so they can attend church together. Mom sings and cries there; the music touches Mom's soul and that alters her mood. After the service, they go for breakfast and Mom talks about her worries and fears for James. Those feelings burden her so. She knows why Franklin stays away. She calls him, but they don't talk very long.

Kisha asks her Mom why the family is so crazy and yet she is successful. All her Mom can say is that Kisha's grandmother acted crazy like James. She would become so angry at the slightest problem that the kids would run for cover. She was mean and got fired from several jobs. None of her kids wanted to visit her. Everyone thought she acted out of sorrow. Her favorite brother had completed suicide at age 22 and her parents had divorced when she was just 13. Life was bitter for Grandma, but she did little to make it better for her children.

Comments on the Story
Some evidence exists that bipolar disorder is genetic. Tracing the extended family's history may reveal that some blood relatives drank a lot, some were diagnosed with bipolar disorder, and at least one relative completed suicide. Kisha's extended family revealed many bipolar symptoms.

Living with family chaos causes strained, if not broken, relationships. In Kisha's family, Grandma offered little stability. Her challenges to offer a secure home were troublesome. When stress filled the home, Grandma lost it. She raged, served charred food, and left the kids behind while she went for long walks. Kisha's Mom worked diligently to improve her own children's lives. Nevertheless, some good and bad family dynamics simply are passed down from generation to generation. "That's just how Mom or Dad would have done it" can be heard in most families.

In Kisha's family, James now controls the family with his bipolar disorder. Several months out of the year, because of his lack of money, he moves back to his mother's home. He spends hours staring at his laptop screen, drinks excessively, screams at his mother and behaves stubbornly. These cause anger, fear and pain for family members. Such a home environment makes Franklin's choice of simply staying away an understandable survival choice.

Kisha has escaped her family's curse. She holds a steady job that she really likes, loves Sam, meets with her younger brother and regularly attends church. These four support systems keep her safely away from the dynamics of Mom's house. Kisha even chose a college far from home to isolate herself from her family. Job availability brought her back. Nevertheless, she rarely sees her mother outside of church and plans to rarely see James.

Kisha's pastor, who knows of the family's situation and has repeatedly spoken with both Kisha and Franklin, recommends that they seek counseling. Both of them decline and believe church will serve the same purpose.

Spiritual Reflection

Kisha and Franklin read the Bible almost every day and sometimes pray together over the phone. They frequently agree to read the same psalm and talk about it at a coffee shop. The last one they discussed was Psalm 42. They found the two verses, beginning with the phrase, "Why are you cast down, oh my soul," compelling. But what brought tears to their eyes was the last verse: "Every day Yahweh, you ordain your love toward me, and during the night you bring me your song, In my prayers to the God of my life."

Kisha and Franklin turn to Bible study for affirmation of God's faithfulness. With this belief, they know their walk through family hurt and pain will not be carried alone. God's presence will undergird them and feed their souls until Sunday's church service or their next time together.

Having a chronic health problem strengthens some people's faith; for others, faith dissolves into negative thoughts and feelings toward God become cynical. Hope dies. Or rather, hope abates. When a flicker of healing occurs, the "divine spark" of hope once again can be ignited. That is what "loving kindness" is all about. One's soul may be "downcast," but God does not leave anyone behind.

Besides church, Kisha and Franklin meet with friends in a cozy room at the nearby library. Each person comes to the Wednesday evening "Together Is Better" support group for those who are affected by a loved one's chronic illness. These fruitful times undergird each person to ignite faltering strength, to blow wind on a dollop of hope, and to refresh members' memories that the group offers love and understanding. People come back every week because they feel that one is never alone.

Kisha's Prayer

Jesus, lead the way. Thank you for the faith connection I have with Franklin and for the love Sam gives me each day. Life is different for James. He is so difficult and hurts me and the whole family — never any ease. I know he suffers and feels lost. He won't listen to anyone. I pray some day he may listen to you. Amen.

LAURA

The Story

The Sandia Mountain range walls in the east side of the flat terrain of Albuquerque, New Mexico. Only on the clearest day can one see the rugged mountains. Driving there takes several hours.

Laura has travelled across five states with her three children: Lars, just beginning to walk; Kaley, who will begin kindergarten in the fall; and Shawn, approaching his seventh birthday. Laura and the kids made the trek to celebrate Grandma Shirley's 83rd birthday and her new apartment. Shirley wants her birthday present to be a family outing the highest point of the Sandias. Laura is eager to oblige her. This trip may be the last time her mother will see the magic of viewing the city lights from the heavens. Laura wants to give her mother this special memory. She also wants her kids to explore a mountain trail.

Laura's father, an avid camper during his lifetime, told his children from their earliest years that one cannot look at *National Geographic* pictures of a mountain and believe one understands a mountain. Rather, a person must view it from a distance, count the hours to reach the mountain and then touch its surface. Laura plans to do just that with her children and her mom. She feels super.

On the drive up the twisted road to the top of the mountain, everyone's ears pop. The kids laugh and then go back to singing Disney songs and eating their snacks. Laura becomes angry at their lack of "mountain magic" and tells them to watch the changes in vegetation. They ignore her. She pulls off the road at a slight shoulder, grabs the snacks and throws them out the window. Grandma sits quietly – and anxiously. Laura resumes driving and lecturing. The children squirm.

After parking the car in the farthest corner of the lot, Laura straps Lars onto her back and directs the other two children to walk in front of her. Grandma walks behind the group. Laura chooses a "medium difficulty" path so everyone can fully experience mountain terrain. After a stretch of minor turns in the path, Laura notices the course's dramatic change. So does Grandma. The path has narrowed to a single lane. Rocks cross over twisted roots. To Laura's joy, she comes upon a fifteen-foot drop-off on her left and a great rock wall hemming them in on the right. Grandma becomes concerned and yells to Laura that the path is getting too dangerous for her grandchildren. Laura finds the comment frivolous. She ignores Shirley's comments and wonders whether her mother's health is failing.

As she hikes, Laura sings loudly. She is thrilled that her kids are here in God's great creation -- a memory for a lifetime. If Laura bothered to look, she would discover that her mother has fallen behind and is nowhere to be seen. But Laura only looks forward. She glances at Shawn, who borrowed extra-big cowboy boots and now is running full speed ahead. His younger sister is not far behind. Laura abruptly stops as she hears Kaley scream. She has tripped on a root and fallen face down. Laura runs to her, sees her bleeding knees, gives her a quick hug and tells her that the inevitable scar will just remind her of this "cherished" mountain climb with Grandma. Laura couldn't be happier.

It starts to drizzle. In no time the path turns slippery and dangerous. Laura lifts her arms to the sky and shouts, "Today is a day the Lord has made. Rejoice and be glad in it." A moment later, Shawn slips on the mud and falls near the trail's drop-off. Laura laughs. Pleased with herself, she thinks that now he really knows a mountain -- its very texture. The drizzle turns into a downpour. Laura stares down the ravine. The children look frightened and confused. They begin to cry. The baby on Laura's back wails. Laura just wants them all to be quiet.

Shirley, even though she is worried about her daughter and grandchildren, returns to the car when the trail becomes too difficult for her. She waits a bit, hoping they will join her. When they don't, she waves down a park ranger and tells him that her grandchildren could be in danger. It is not the first time Shirley has feared for her grandchildren's safety and called for help.

The ranger carefully steps along the rugged path and finds Laura and the children crouched under an overhang. He takes the two older ones to their grandmother, who stands under a tree at the beginning of the path. Laura – embarrassed by the rescue and irritated with her mother's interference -- emerges with the baby firmly secured to her back.

As they walk to the car, Laura can sense her mother's unspoken criticism. "Happy birthday Mom," Laura mockingly whispers. "I hope you enjoyed your birthday at the top of the mountain. It sure was fun meeting the park patrol guy."

As they drive down the mountain, no one says much.

Comments on the Story

Laura did not intend to scare her children and put them at risk. She loved them. Looking at the mountain path, most parents would not have taken young children on a "medium difficulty" hike. But Laura was not like most parents. Her inability to discern potential danger and control her impulsivity repeatedly placed her and her children in harm's way.

When Laura was a child, Shirley patched up her bloody knees and elbows. Several wounds turned into scars. But Laura played hockey, fast-pitch softball and volleyball. Bruises and cuts were to be expected, but some could not be explained by sports injuries. Laura had an individual "sport" that resulted in bruises. She taunted younger kids. She would humiliate them by pulling them to her, calling them names and finally engaging them in fistfights. Parents complained to the principal and demanded that the school intervene. As required, the principal called Shirley and yet another conference would address Laura's abusive behaviors. Shirley felt overwhelmed by her daughter's extreme behavior. What could she do? Nothing. Laura lived in her own world.

Shirley knew where Laura lived -- inside her locked bedroom with a chair propped against the door to keep anyone from entering. She stayed up nights worrying about Laura's behavioral issues and fielded telephone calls from the school about her truancy. She repeatedly walked upstairs to stand outside Laura's bedroom and beg her to come out to eat, take a shower or call friends. Laura dismissed her mother's pleas. Mom has been hurt more than Laura will ever know. Shirley thinks maybe she was just a bad mother.

Spiritual Reflection

"God is love." This belief has guided the Judeo-Christian tradition for millennia. Images in the Bible of God's love and protection flow throughout the psalms, creation stories, covenants, prophets and Jesus' ministry.

Today, many churches profess that God loves each person like a parent loves her child. How then do people with bipolar disorder who have placed their loved ones in perilous positions live with the memories of such decisions? When in a stable mood, Laura remembers with horror the danger she has sometimes placed those in her care. Shame and regret stick to her like glue. She understands she has bipolar disorder, but often when she is in hypomania, she only feels happy to be alive.

During those energetic, creative and self-confident times, she loves God and expresses that feeling freely. Yet an internal voice often reverberates in her brain: "If God so loves the world and me, why doesn't God change me so I can be the mom my kids can trust and feel safe with?" Laura wonders whether God created the universe, humanity, a land, a nation and a community of believers and then just left humanity to its own resources. Evidence such as war, famine, disasters and humanity's cruelty could provide a simple answer, "Yes." Other historical events, however, contradict that simple response.

Scripture records many times when God intervened in the human condition to improve people's lives. Biblical examples, however, may be considered irrelevant when one suffers a debilitating illness. But when a person shares with another who is experiencing the same illness -- feelings of self-loathing, despair, loss, fear, aloneness and hopelessness -- this sharing can result in the birth of a faith community. These "holy moments" undergird those involved and such experiences can affect their judgments of humanity and even their judgments of God. Faith in a power greater than each other has the potential gift of offering healings like those found in scripture. Some may even call these moments "miracles."

Often people with bipolar disorder, a serious medical condition, struggle with God. During experiences of increased self-esteem, high energy, rapid thinking, increased productivity, an overactive sex life and delusions of grandeur, God may seem irrelevant. On the other hand, one may express great gratitude to God for such a high quality of life. When depression sets in, feelings of God's abandonment and severe judgment can come crashing down. But when people with bipolar talk with each other about spiritual stories or their experiences of God's presence, healing from deep despair can take place and even ignite that flicker of hope set deep within each person's soul.

Grandmother's Prayer

Lord, I worry. Take this burden from me. My Laura loves her kids -- my grandchildren -- but sometimes she frightens me with her blindness. Her kids get scared. They will learn not to trust their own mom. I know I have contributed to this situation. If I could only go back in time, I would have paid more attention. Now she won't listen to me. We don't talk. I ruined that avenue. I need to give my worries up to you. I also need you to send Laura an angel she can trust. That would be the miracle in my life and a miracle for my daughter and grandchildren. Amen.

Healing is the relief from pain -- physical, emotional, mental or spiritual. No one is saved from illnesses, accidents, crushed relationships or shattered beliefs in some truths that shaped one's life.

Life is difficult. Look around. Everyone has gone through hard times. The miracle of this time in history is that most people can heal. Healing doesn't necessarily mean that one returns to full functioning without pain. Healing can be a cure from a serious illness, relationship reconciliation, freedom from childhood trauma or forgiveness from a deep hurt by another. Healing also can be achieving job satisfaction, implementing financial discipline, securing self-esteem or accepting a mental-health-illness diagnosis. It is also putting in place professional and personal support people to individualize strategies that will offer stability instead of a life of chaos.

For people with bipolar disorder or any of the other three mental disorders -- depression, anxiety and Attention Deficit Hyperactivity (ADHD) -- to choose to heal means facing suffering with wisdom, not from a position of victimization. Living with bipolar is not a death sentence. Living with bipolar is embracing four tools to birth one's "best life."

The tools examined here come from people within the bipolar community: those afflicted with bipolar, family and friends, and professionals committed to serving those with mood disorders. Others in the community include organizations that provide information and support for people with various mental-health illnesses, organizations that lobby for legislation to improve the lives of people with bipolar and other mood disorders, the National Institute of Mental Health and the National Institute on Drug Abuse.

Using information gathered from this community, I have identified four tools directed to those diagnosed with bipolar disorder and their resilient support people in order to fully live in a place of strength, solace and self-advocacy. These tools are:

- Healing with the knowledge that each person with mental illness today is connected with the millions of people from hundreds of generations with mental-health illnesses.

- Healing from the twin warriors of stigma and shame.

- Healing from isolation by acknowledging that one belongs to a welcoming bipolar community and by availing oneself of the resources and services readily available.

- Healing by nurturing one's spiritual life.

The end result of "walking with the four healing tools" is the self-talk of "I have a health problem – not a character defect -- that I can manage with integrity, not perfection."

Tool 1: Healing by understanding those who came before us

Throughout history, people with mental illness and those with feared diseases have suffered hellish treatment. At the same time, researchers have worked to understand the functioning of a broken brain, to use trial-and-error methods to treat the brain, and to implement both recognized treatment protocols as well as new approaches to alleviate suffering. For those in the bipolar community, understanding that they are not alone is essential to healing.

Over the centuries, people crippled by the rages of mental-health illnesses have suffered horrific and barbaric treatment. Without individual choice or personal power, governmental protection, safe shelter or advocates, these suffering souls have been herded into asylums, ostracized by families, mocked, denied functioning communities and judged by political and religious leaders to be rightfully punished for unspeakable sins, demon possession, speaking in tongues or hearing voices.

Mentally ill people were left to live on the streets as beggars or imprisoned in insane asylums, where they received meager amounts of food and clean water, went naked or wore torn and putrid-smelling rags, listened to screams day and night, were chained to posts, steeped in their own urine and feces. Scientists used incarcerated patients for experiments that left them physically ruined. Wardens raped and tortured people and starved them to death. Some prisoners concentrated on finding a way to commit suicide, which could be considered healthy given the cacophony of wailing and screaming by hallucinating and paranoid individuals. Those with manic-depressive illness (today called bipolar disorder) delivered passionate speeches as if they were royalty, the pope or Jesus. Inevitably, they would sink into depression, making them even more vulnerable to abuse.

To illustrate the treatment of the mentally ill, a brief look at the history of one of the world's oldest mental institutions is in order. Bethlem Royal Hospital in London, long referred to as Bedlam, was established in 1247 as the priory of the New Order of St. Mary of Bethlehem. Its purpose initially was to care for the poor and homeless, but over time it came to focus on those labeled "mad." The British government took control of the facility in the 1370s and it came under control of the City of London in 1547. It remained the only public mental institution for another 300 years. Today, the hospital continues to operate -- with state-of-the-art treatment programs.

For its first 200 hundred years, the hospital was funded by a combination of meager public dollars, donations from religious groups and small contributions from families. Much of the money ended up in the pockets of the doctors and administrators, with a pittance going to the staff who provided patient care. When a doctor resigned, he hired a relative or friend to continue the practice of ignoring the patients but keeping the salary. Bedlam had been built over a sewer, which was regularly blocked, allowing waste to seep into the building. Officials inspecting it in 1598 found it to be "filthily kept." A subsequent inspection found starving inmates. A staff person known as the "Keeper" was charged with the daily tasks of feeding the patients and keeping the hospital operating. He also stole money earmarked by the government to meet basic needs of the patients. The powerless patients were left vulnerable to his desires.

By the eighteenth century, European intellectuals were challenging the cultural status quo and concern for the mentally ill became an agenda for change. To improve the care for those with mental illnesses, the cultural elite influenced elected officials to establish more private and public hospitals. This brought better treatment to those in private hospitals, which had more financial resources – including contributions from families -- to serve their patients with trained staff, respected medical researchers and trained doctors. Public hospitals such as Bedlam, on the other hand, received less money, provided less care and were less respected. There, the barbaric routines of the past remained the norm.

One unsettling routine was the use of Bedlam as a source of amusement. Dignitaries, public officials and community leaders received special invitations to witness the patients' "bizarre" behaviors and sounds. It wasn't long before the townspeople learned of this, and soon they would go to the hospital and pay a penny to watch "the freaks." Also during this time, people in the pubs and on street corners sold ditties making fun of the mentally ill. One example is "Love's Lunacie," subtitled "Mad Besses Fegary" [prank]. Its introductory words explain that a young man named Tom did the maiden Besse "some wrong," which prompted her to write a song. It begins:

Mad Besse, so they call me,
I'm metamorphosed;
Strange sights and visions I do see,
By Furies I am led.
Tom was the cause of all my woe,
To him I loudly cry,
My love to him there's none doth know,
Yet here he lets me lie.

She goes on to describe her life in Bedlam, including this stanza:

This Bethlem is a place of torment;
Here's fearful notes still sounding;
Here minds are filled with discontent,
And terrors still abounding.
Some shake their chains in woeful wise,
Some swear, some curse, some roaring,
Some shrieking out with fearful cries,
And some their cloths are tearing.

Likewise, artists captured the imprisoned life of the mentally ill. For example, in the early nineteenth century, one of Francisco Jose de Goya's last canvasses was "Casa de locos" (The Madhouse).

While many "commoners" mocked the mentally ill, the well-educated people of the Enlightenment encouraged and supported legislation that produced oversight of hospitals and money to support vigorous research based on case studies of patients living in private hospitals. Such research paved the way from barbaric treatment of the mentally ill to an understanding of various mental illnesses, operating safe housing, initiating new treatment modalities and testing medications to find those that would reduce mental pain. Four preeminent researchers whose work birthed the core of hope, healing and spirit must be acknowledged.

The Greek physician Hippocrates (460-337 BCE) is considered one of the most outstanding figures in the world of medicine. Indeed, the medical world calls him the "father of medicine." His legacy evolved from the quality of his research and, equally important, the ethics of his work. "First do no harm" -- the well-known phrase associated with physicians -- has its origins in his "The History of Epidemics."

Hippocrates' patients lived on palatial hospital grounds, not chained to immoveable objects. He observed them, wrote copious notes and prescribed herbs and a balanced diet to treat those with mental-health illnesses. His research differed from popular treatments of the time -- appeasing the gods, ingesting fluids of unknown origin, turning to philosophers for explanations -- and was the benchmark of future medical study.

The second preeminent researcher is Wilhelm Griesinger, a renowned pioneer of German scientific psychiatry, who concluded that many mental illnesses are treatable and some are curable. Griesinger's work in the early nineteenth century motivated ethical managers of insane asylums to divide their patients into groups -- those who were treatable, those who were curable and those who were not mentally ill. This was important because treatable patients received the most intensive case management. Curable people could be given the attention necessary to transition to treatment protocols. And those imprisoned for reasons other than mental illness could be released.

The third man, German psychiatrist Emil Kraepelin, is the most recognized researcher of manic-depressive disorder in the early twentieth century. He researched the connections between brain biology and mental illness. After years of observing patients and writing detailed case studies that included notes on their symptoms, Kraepelin identified groups with a pattern of euphoria and depression. He prescribed morphine to mitigate symptoms, modified dosages and insured regular ingestion of it. This protocol remarkably improved the lives of people with mood swings. His detailed case studies and his treatment modalities furnished subsequent researchers with a depth of knowledge from which they could launch their own scientific work.

In a long list of determined researchers, John Cade deserves recognition for his pharmaceutical contributions. In the 1940s, using his kitchen as his laboratory, Cade found that lithium chloride, a natural salt, sedated his guinea pigs. He gave this salt to psychotics and they, too, experienced fewer hallucinations. Cade's work received international acclaim and other scientists began research trials. The salt was found to have negative side effects, and by the 1960s a new drug – lithium -- replaced lithium chloride. Lithium became the standard medication for bipolar disorder.

In summary, focusing on the history of treatment of the mentally ill may be a catalyst for individuals in the bipolar community to understand that the manic-depressive illness is a very old illness with an ugly past. Because of their attention to the mistreatment of its victims, committed researchers over the centuries studied people with extreme mood changes and tested treatment modalities and compounds to lessen or eliminate this mood disease. Today, those in the bipolar community need not feel alone, unimportant or discarded. Rather, people now can rely on professional diagnosis, efficacious medication, various options of talk therapy and dedicated support people to manage their disorder and live their "best life."

Tool 2: Healing from the twin warriors of stigma and shame
Stigma is the judgment from others that a person has a physical, intellectual or emotional difference that makes her a target of discrimination. One can see the birth of stigma when a child is the last chosen for a game, rejected by a study group or called names on the school bus. These vulnerable children experience isolation, mean-spirited comments and bullying. It is no wonder that people fear stigma. It smells rancid from the rotted words and judgments of others.

It is true that many individuals have told their stories of living with bipolar disorder. Numerous organizations have spent millions of dollars educating the general population about bipolar and depression. Each effort contributes enormous kindness to those stigmatized and stuck in dark places. Yet many people with mental-health illnesses remain undiagnosed and untreated. It is difficult to solve this problem because they look like our neighbor, the person in the next cubicle at work, the student in a calculus class, the dog-walker, the mother of a small child or an executive of a Fortune 500 company. Likewise, for such individuals to confide in a friend, boss, sibling, or trusted church member risks unexpected exposure. The forces of stigma can come crashing down and with them shame. So stigma comes down to an individual making decisions about who to trust. If one chooses to speak of his or her illness, the consequences of miscalculating can result in facing stigma's omnipresent twin: shame.

Shame can be described as a whole-body experience that includes feeling exposed to others as being bad, ugly, awful, no good. Most people will do anything to avoid shame and will go to great lengths to find a way to deflect its power. Others respond in self-defense with anger, tears or silence. Still others simply accept the judgments as the definition of their self-worth.

In her story, Emily is dealing with stigma and shame. In childhood, she experienced a multitude of tests to determine what was "wrong" with her. Classmates noticed the many times Emily was pulled from classes to see the counselor. They teased her and called her names like "stupid" and "weird." These words crushed Emily; no one could protect her from the inevitable shame. In young adulthood, she faced the stresses of a new environment at college and the challenges of demanding academic work and a new set of friends. Later, she experienced mood changes while active in her community (hypomania and depression), divorced, attempted suicide and ended up in a hospital psych unit. Each of these occurrences carried with it stigma and shame for Emily and also for her family and friends. Who stuck by Emily throughout these public humiliations? No one. Those closest to her tried, but bipolar disorder can exhaust even the most-committed support people.

For those with bipolar or other mental-health illness, like Emily, stigma and shame inflame suffering in the body, mind, emotions and soul. These wounds can be examined by considering two distinctive types of suffering: *"innate suffering"* and *"consequential suffering."*

"Innate suffering" is the private reflection one enters into upon receiving a diagnosis of bipolar disorder and during the process of accepting the diagnosis. The concept of living one's life stuck with a mental disability that one did not choose, desire, value or invite into one's life can be daunting. One cannot escape the parade of questions, feelings and attitudes about the label "mental illness." A myriad of scary, negative and foreboding images pop into one's mind. Within this collage, negative words or pictures dominate. One is forced to stare stigma and shame in the face.

Other diseases, equally difficult to manage and also requiring daily attention, such as childhood diabetes, may be received with fear and trepidation. But when people hear "bipolar," fear and trepidation are likely just the first of a long list of words describing their reaction to the diagnosis.

It is important to note that for some, receiving a diagnosis of bipolar gives comfort. When one's world has been filled with chaos, failure, slipping self-esteem, guilt and rejection, a diagnosis that places destructive symptoms under one roof brings a feeling of ease, comfort and empowerment. A disease -- not personal character -- is the cause of all those actions that fill a toxic storage container of regrets. A disease can be treated.

Accepting a diagnosis of a mental illness can take years. Too many people never believe the diagnosis or avail themselves of services that would relieve or minimize the bipolar symptoms ruling their lives. Divorce decrees include references to mental-health illness. Relapses in twelve-step programs point to the failure of self-medicating. Custody battles include the destructive nature of the disorder. Health-care costs reflect unnecessary emergency-room use as well as hospital stays resulting from dangerous behaviors gone wrong. And frantic families call 9-1-1 because of an attempted or completed suicide.

For the great majority of people, hearing the word "bipolar" is tantamount to telling someone he has fourth-stage cancer. The rebellion against the diagnosis many times is based on the expectation of stigma that will limit their choices and options in life. And following right behind is the shame that they are "less than" other people. Sometimes they reject the diagnosis with the familiar words "not me" and return to a routine of self-medicating their moods.

This "innate suffering" is not a passive process that will produce magical answers. Bipolar can be volatile, and knowing one's vulnerabilities can prepare the afflicted person to seize control and manage situations that could be detrimental to one's family, professional obligations and social life.

Newly diagnosed people typically will look back through the years and identify times of envious high self-esteem, high energy followed by terrible failures, escalating anger, judging people and calling them to accountability. Often other memories quickly come to mind that define the depressive mood. Alienating people, hating oneself, treating people with impatience, spiking to quick-witted anger, lying on the couch not very interested in life – all these are examples of the self-punishment that bipolar inflicts upon individuals.

Identifying one's patterns, triggers, symptoms and past attempts at relieving symptoms requires hours of reflection. Repeatedly going over one's angers and other destructive feelings eventually allows a person to make peace with the picture of his unique life with bipolar. It brings forth important information that will enhance personal management of the disorder and allow for early intervention to prevent a slide into more serious symptom expressions.

A major processing question after learning that one lives with a complex and difficult illness is the omnipresent "Why me?" Few people pass through "innate suffering," with its baggage of stigma and shame, without asking that question. There is no one answer. Some of those who teach and research on bipolar disorder and other mental illnesses agree that there is a genetic disposition to the disorder. Some of those with bipolar talk about a "crazy" relative or a sibling or parent dragged down by bipolar. Psychiatrists also have determined that some people with Post-Traumatic Stress Disorder will be diagnosed with bipolar disorder. And from all the stories psychiatrists hear, sometimes the "Why me?" can only be answered with, "Just bad luck."

Experts at the National Institute of Mental Health suggest that answers are right around the corner, that new research soon will speak to the complexity of the causes of bipolar disorder. For those feeling tainted, isolated, confused and angry, however, these researchers still live in the "ivory tower of academia." Other afflicted people understand the "Why me?" question as a spiritual question. In their despair, with the reality that they have a tough life, they wonder, "Where are you, God, in my suffering?" Theologians have spent more than two thousand years wrestling with this question. Opinions differ vastly. The root question behind an individual's plea is the nature of God. Put another way, how does each person define God?

Within "innate suffering," one truth seems to be unvoiced. Each individual dealing with bipolar disorder and other mental-health illnesses spends a lifetime "wondering-worrying." Did her bipolar cause her to lose a promotion or was the other person more qualified? Was his anger justified or a trigger for a possible mood change? Was she making everyone at the party laugh because she is naturally an extrovert or was she hypomanic?

This "wondering-worrying" comes from the fear of stigma and the abhorrent fear of shame. "Innate suffering" conceptualizes the multitude of self-conversations about each person's unique bipolar symptoms, triggers and time variations of bipolar expression. These conversations erupt many times over the years.

Bipolar is not a mild disease accompanied by loved ones' consistent support, family unity, sympathetic employers or the delivery of a friend's tuna casserole. Bipolar rips apart many of the expectations people hold about normal human behaviors and relationships. Life with bipolar leaves a trail of destruction, chaos and nagging regret. People are hurt beyond endurance. Alcohol and drugs are misused for self-medication. Multiple divorces are common. Children grow to adulthood without safety. Employers face higher health insurance costs because of the drain of hospitalizations, out-patient treatments, medications and professional services by doctors and therapists.

People with bipolar disorder know that if they could control their moods they would. If they could rein in behaviors that bring pain to others or themselves, they would. Joseph's story demonstrates this.

When Joseph organized his birthday party, he bought all the food and drink necessary for people to feel welcomed and happy to be at his house to celebrate with him. Weeks before his birthday, however, Joseph had decided to get off his medication, which made him vulnerable to a mood swing. And that is what happened. The stress of preparations overwhelmed Joseph and just hours before his party he was on the couch. When Molly, his new love, arrived to help him, Joseph was so consumed by an attack on his self-esteem that he refused to answer the door. Molly finally walked away wondering, "Really, who is this guy?" Days later Joseph knew he had two choices -- avoid the guests he had invited or mend fences. Because a party is typically not a deal breaker among friends, Joseph could come up with some believable lie or tell people what happened to him because of his bipolar. The far more difficult problem was how to gain Molly's trust.

The side effects of bipolar disorder can be as "mild" as Joseph's party or as extreme as Emily's lifelong battle with mood disorders. Innate suffering is not passive. The mind reaches into dark places and explores treacherous ground. This suffering is often unexplainable to others. Some people say, "Pull yourself up by your bootstraps" or "Pray for your suffering to go away." But chemistry is powerful. And self-revealing is risky.

Unlike the private innate suffering, *consequential suffering* is played out in the public arena. Bipolar is not a "nice" disease. Diagnosed people hurt, dismiss, insult, judge, scare and love people involved in their lives. A great blessing occurs when someone with bipolar realizes the relationship damage she has caused to significant people in her life. Screaming at a child, swearing at a parent, slamming the boss' door, not showing up as the maid of honor at a best friend's wedding -- these behaviors are a few examples of cruel actions. These jarring offenses become evident in the eyes of deeply hurt, burdened and scared support people.

As periods of mood stability elongate and believability of sustained stability develops into a rocky road to trust, the need for reconciliation in meaningful relationships becomes evident. Redeeming oneself requires a series of sincere apologies, continuous trustworthy behaviors and making amends to those most devastated by events. Sometimes conversations that shed light on particularly painful incidents, sharing stories of other people's experiences in support groups, and attentiveness to others' need brings understanding, forgiveness and renewed commitments to remain part of a support network. Too many times, though, such actions turn out to be insufficient. Then, for example, divorce papers are served, children are taken to live in a safer home, friends burn out. Other support people cannot find a way to escape.

For example, Beatrice, her love for a spouse long deadened from abuse, feels trapped. She can't leave Harold. He has lost all his support people, including his adult son. Without Beatrice, Harold would be on the streets. Beatrice cannot be so cruel, even though each day Harold dismisses her as a problem, failing to see the angel he has at his side. In his story, Hank shows a way to redemption. Hank has carved out a good life for himself and Stone, his trusted dog. He also keeps in contact with his father who, Hank believes, saved his life. Yet Hank had a huge hurt in his heart. He ran out on his sons when they were in grade school and did not reach out to them for nearly two decades. His reflection during his "innate suffering" pointed to a plan to rectify the ruin in the "consequential suffering."

That plan involved inviting his sons and their families to join him up north. Hank believed that sharing stories around a fire pit would give healing a chance. Hank began by apologizing and telling his kids they did nothing to deserve his punishments. He repeatedly told them they were not to blame or held any responsibility. The boys were relieved. These conversations continued for a few days, and upon leaving, his sons asked to spend more time with him. Hank believed that request was a blessing, a gift -- and another chance at reconciliation. He now lives on solid ground. It is his and Stone's job to keep it so.

Redemption, after a few intentional acts to re-establish relationships, will not be accomplished with a few hunting trips, however. Hank's life is filled with decisions that caused much pain and anguish for his family, employers and friends. Redemption for Hank will be long and hard. The one angel who stuck with him was his father, John, who never condemned Hank or shamed him for his bad decisions. John had dealt with loved ones with a mental-health illness. He knew the ropes. He never lost faith that Hank could turn his life around. John was Hank's only support person. Sometimes it takes only one; the third tool for healing is establishing a support system that looks a lot like John.

Tool 3: Healing with help

One can think about a support person or caregiver as one who assists a vulnerable person. Because we all are vulnerable people, we all depend on others to help us along the way, be it an intimate partner, friend, co-worker, neighbor or teacher. Many people live in gratefulness for their support system. These "best friends" stand with us on "holy ground." Also important are those people who lend their support with a kind gesture, such as sending a card, sharing memories of vacations or going to the movies. Not all support needs to be hard work.

Primary support people for those with bipolar disorder can be categorized by the services they provide. One group, the professionally trained specialist, includes psychiatrists, therapists, social workers, religious/spiritual confidants, teachers and nurses. A second group is comprised of intimate partners, family members, friends, co-workers and others with mental-health illnesses. A third group -- the "tough love" support people -- make difficult decisions when a person with bipolar exhibits bizarre behavior and may hurt himself or others. All three groups offer relationship, not abandonment.

Life for a person with bipolar is better and safer with support people. Each defines her/his support networks differently. Some choose only professional people to care for them. Others add spouse-partner-boyfriend-girlfriend-significant other. Most persons with bipolar establish a support network that provides task-oriented support. The people in this network carry a heavy load of responsibilities, and their tasks can be comforting for the person with bipolar -- or controlling.

They may accompany the person to doctors' appointments to be a second set of ears, to develop plans to deal with stress or even determine when the person needs hospitalization. Such support people may organize medications to reduce the probability of non-use as well as over-use. Other tasks may include monitoring moods and sleep patterns, pacing activities to reduce stress, and implementing strategies to reduce the possibility of a full-blown episode.

When the person won't get off the couch for days, spits out venomous words, declares her grandiosity, lavishly spends money needed for bills, ignores employment responsibilities or threatens those around her, much is required of the "tough love" caregivers. One or two people need to be the psych-unit contacts. They must be available for meetings to discuss treatment options. They may need to spend time watching educational videos. They will find themselves repeatedly talking to the patient regarding details of the treatment protocols. And, as a high priority, they will visit the patient. Bringing an item of want or listening to his psych-unit experiences reduces anxiety for the patient and promotes better self-care. These acts of kindness cradle the person in hope and not the clutches of despair. Other support people will tend to the practical jobs that must get done. Usually the care of children ranks first on the list of needs. Other jobs include calling family and friends, taking care of pets, paying bills, cleaning and canceling social or professional commitments. As weeks pass, decisions are placed with the person with bipolar, who now is functioning much better because medications have been modified and proven effective and/or ECTs have provided relief. Witnessing the patient's healing fuels the power of hope for all involved. The return to health is celebrated.

This example illustrates a near-perfect scenario. But many people with mental-health illness have less of a support network. The hospitalized person has a few tired and discouraged relatives and friends. Some support people may need this crisis to pass without their involvement. At times, the hospitalized person may have no "tough love" support people. The medical team and social services fill this gap. Often, these new faces offer necessary and compassionate care.

From the perspective of some people with bipolar, living locked in a psych unit feels a lot like the last bad time, and they may smirk at the thought that hope is an innate power that holds a steady rudder. However, the person needs to see evidence: Support people showed up to help out, just as they did the last time.

It is often said that support people lead a "tough life." Anecdotes, as well as data from my thesis study, which included people with bipolar disorder (Participants), Professionals and Caregivers, support such a statement. It was particularly telling that two out of ten Participants left unmarked any question relating to their support network. None of the Participants attended a support group. In more than 200 possible responses from Participants, only one person wrote complimentary opinions about support people. An exact interpretation for these responders cannot be made, but is reasonable to conclude that some people with bipolar lack empathy.

Caregivers, on the other hand, repeatedly wrote empathic comments about their afflicted person. The study also revealed that support people suffer from the criticism and negative judgments Participants expressed about their Caregivers. The logical question that follows this data is, "Why would anyone stay in such a relationship?" The answers vary. Some Caregivers love their spouse, partner, boy/girl friend, sibling, parent or friend. Even though they may hear hurtful words, those words are not a sufficient reason to break a vow they made. But staying together comes at a cost to the Caregivers, who remember past behaviors that were hurtful and damaging to their well-being. They feel trapped, manipulated, dismissed or victimized.

A look at Kisha's story illustrates the complex demands made of a support person. She helps her very troubled brother, James, who has bipolar, with countless tasks. She takes her mother to church every Sunday, after which they go to breakfast and talk about bipolar. Besides her full-time job, she has an intimate relationship with Sam, who has decided he cannot be around James. Kisha's other brother, Franklin, will not join the family for any reason, so she regularly calls him. They also attend a Bible study group comprised of people facing major family issues.

Some support people are not even aware of the role they play -- or their significant contribution. A teacher takes extra time to help a student. A coach notices a change in behaviors and alerts a parent. A postal worker sees that a person has not picked up mail in several days and so rings the bell to hand it over. A coworker observes that her neighbor in the next cubicle is having a bad day and asks him to lunch.

In short, the circle of support people is endless. Each support person is vital and indispensable. Each helps the person with mental-health illness to live a richer and safer life.

Tool 4: Healing by nurturing one's spiritual life
Sometimes an individual needs to call her best friend, plant a raspberry bush, read the Bible, listen to music, walk in the woods, meditate, write in a journal or just focus on breathing. One's spirit requires attention to keep her open to love -- of herself, a special person or God.

When a person feels empty, un-centered, disconnected in relationships or pressured from stress, his spirit falls back into someplace called "later." Sometimes "later" means weeks, months or years. One's emotional, intellectual or physical well-being is out of balance or has been depleted.

An empty tank just makes every day more difficult. Self-esteem suffers, relationships weaken, bad habits increase, and blaming others for minor mishaps dominates one's thinking. Self-care becomes weaker.

Whether one believes in God or not, a person's spirit is independent from church doctrine, dogma or voices from family members who believe they know the one way to find spiritual fulfillment. For people with bipolar disorder, nurturing their spirit sets their feet on solid ground and makes managing the distressing disorder clearer and easier. They now have a connected inner life that thwarts impulsivity, tones down anger, suffocates self-deprecation, blocks the blows of others' judgments and allows them to breathe.

I know my spirit is depleted when I wake in the night with negative and scary thoughts, repeat regretful stories as if they happened just last week, talk incessantly, dismiss people important to me, work at multiple projects without finishing any or get impatient with my dog. With these behaviors, my God has been silenced and my giving to others forgotten.

Belly laughs, prolonged hugs, mindfully appreciating those whom we love and who love us, watching less television, intimate conversations and taking time to talk with the power greater than ourselves -- these sorts of things give us inner peace. Living with ourselves in peace may be the standard by which we know that all is well with our soul and we are in balance.

Bipolar disorder, depression, anxiety or Attention Deficit Hyperactivity will not have the last word. They may occupy paragraphs during symptom elevation, but they do not tell the whole story. These mood disorders do not dominate our lives, and we do not need to live in their shadows, waiting for the next eruption. We are fine people most of the time. So is everyone else.

My Story

My story of healing is simple: I saw a psychiatrist five days after I told a cherished friend who worked in a mental-health/chemical-dependency clinic of my scary behaviors. I recounted examples of escalating high-risk behaviors coupled with cutting comments to friends, impatient snipes at restaurant servers for minor mistakes, outrageous behavior at school, critical judgments of others and over-the-edge happiness. I wondered if my problem could be explained as too much stress -- three young children not getting enough of me and attending graduate school part-time. At the conclusion of our conversation, my friend suggested that I meet with a doctor in her clinic.

Five days later, I sat face-to-face with a psychiatrist. We talked about my present life. It wasn't long before I realized that he knew all the stories I had told my friend. Relief flooded over me; I had no interest in confessing embarrassing stories to a stranger. He asked me simple questions in a light-hearted manner. He asked me to use a computer to answer questions. After he had a chance to read the printout and review his notes, he said matter-of-factly, "You have bipolar disorder. It can be treated with medication." Whoa, I didn't expect this! That day I started taking lithium. Follow-up appointments were scheduled -- one week, two weeks, four weeks, three months -- to closely monitor the effects of the medication.

As I review that life-changing day, I realize my doctor provided me three services: a listening ear to determine a diagnosis, medication to stabilize my moods and a rigid schedule of appointments. Like the three-legged birthing chair I treasure, these services provided stability and a solid foundation for new life.

Besides his role as medication specialist, at those appointments my doctor listened for indications of my increased quality of life and side effects of the lithium. He recommended I regularly see a therapist knowledgeable in mood disorders. He explained the importance of regular appointments in order to reduce stress, identify triggers, problem-solve issues, accept the diagnosis and build self-esteem.

His final recommendation in this first chapter of managing my disorder included my attending a Depression/Bipolar Support Alliance group. He explained that participation in a group specifically aimed at people with bipolar would give me the opportunity to learn about the disorder, hear stories that I could compare with my own experiences and meet others who have faced difficult times and made healthy decisions. He also said the group would be a good sounding board for my questions, frustrations and situations, and would allow me to help others by sharing my experiences. Bottom line: group participation would help me see that I am not the only person with the disorder and that whatever situation I am trying to resolve, someone in the group had a similar story.

I attended these groups for several years and credit the participants with giving me the tools to deal with stigma, with the difficult journey of acceptance of my disorder, and with believing I am not "bipolar" -- it's just an aspect of my life. Today, I still return to a group when I feel my foundation eroding.

During my first few months of doctor appointments, I learned five important pieces of information in order to self direct my care: my diagnosis, reliable medication, the importance of monitoring my moods, the need for a therapist, and the importance of support, whether groups or individuals. My support groups consisted of DBSA members, my husband, my graduate-school faculty advisor and cherished friends.

After twenty-five years managing my disorder, I am grateful for that support system. I know that my family and dear friends love me. I am gifted every day with the consistent knowledge that I am appreciated, respected and fun. This quality of life, however, does not mean these lovely people understand many of my behaviors that fall under the rubric of bipolar disorder. They rarely recognize my inappropriate behaviors -- quick judgments, rudeness, super ideas, anxiety, unreliability, impatience, short-fuse anger -- as expressions of my disorder. Rather, I hear judgments about the nature of my character or personality faults. Without doubt, I act in ways that embarrass me and will have negative consequences for me. I know that means I must add more people to the countless number of folks I have already apologized to this year. Shame still enters my life on a regular basis. When I get strong, I soothe myself by saying for the thousandth time, "They just don't get it." I wish it were different.

Also, like most people with bipolar disorder, I deal with other mental-health issues. Eighty percent of us also live with ADHD, and it is not unusual for anxiety to be added to the mix. To further complicate life, other significant health issues -- typical of the general population – often must be addressed. So living the "best life" requires consistent management of mood disorders, full attention to the diagnosis of other health issues and strict compliance to dramatically increase the successful healing from these problems.

Sometimes the demands of managing it all feel overwhelming, and the requirements of life drain our energy. What we must do is give ourselves some slack, get involved in pleasurable activities, take "alone time" and spend time with positive people who know how to laugh. We must remember that for many people – not just those with bipolar disorder -- life at times *is* exhausting.

Thus it is that with my healing I have come to realize that even during trying times, new life awaits me. The three foundations of my healing remain firmly in place. My family and "sisters" take turns standing at the back of my metaphorical birthing chair prepared to offer support. I sit in the chair and place my feet in the holes provided for me to give birth. The midwives are the spirits of God prepared to call out "new life" -- over and over again. The chair cannot be broken or worn out. That's what is wonderful about the birthing chair -- it's stable, it's well used and it's holy.

Spirit

Ann & Charlie

The Story

Ann, 41, begins her first day as a retail consultant at a major national chain; it's her third assignment in five years. The company's management cannot ignore her productivity, far above that of her colleagues. They keep her in order to meet other departments' sinking sales. When her behavior threatens any department's stability and reputation, she is shipped off to another store far away.

Ann has suitors. Most of her affairs are with co-workers, but every once in awhile a customer responds to her blatant flirting. Ann just enjoys her playful times. She laughs, feels light, acts bravely, risks all for the attention that touches her overwhelming energy. Relief comes only when she shuts another man's door. The next day her appetite searches for another dessert. Charlie, her husband, appears not to notice.

With two adopted girls from India, ages seven and nine, Charlie does not want to endanger the family's stability given the children's disruptive past. Charlie knows of some of Ann's adventures but feels trapped in a corner. He suspects Ann will be hunting when she asks more of him, both with the kids and in the bedroom. Charlie takes over all parenting responsibilities. The children get delightful new toys, invite more friends home, do less schoolwork, play more video games and visit their much-loved grandparents.

Charlie struggles with his enabling, and when Ann's episodes cease he thinks about the patterns of the previous weeks. He is angry and feels betrayed. He punishes Ann with cutting words and condescending stares. He wishes he could get back on his career path. But Ann makes so much more money than he could and they move so frequently. Charlie tells himself and those he meets that he is a stay-at-home dad. People tell him how wonderful that is.

In the still of the night, Charlie reads scripture, prays and wrestles with God. He begs for the strength to forgive himself as well as Ann. He deeply loves his wife and pleads to God that Ann will stop bringing so much pain to the family.

Charlie needs time to think and feels overwhelmed. He wonders how long it will be before Ann's behavior at work means pulling the children out of their school, moving to a new city, adjusting to different classes and establishing new friends. Fortunately, the girls are familiar with a few military families, so moving about seems natural. Charlie hates the change. Again he turns to God and pleads that there will be no more moves.

Comments on the Story

Neither Ann nor Charlie admits that Ann has significant problems. Charlie denies, the kids suspect and Ann enjoys. Her flings only last a few weeks; none of the characters come to the family home. In pain, Charlie desperately turns to God in anger, tears and confusion. He wants answers but God remains silent. Charlie believes God is punishing him because his forgiveness of Ann is not rock solid, and he suffers from guilt because of his bedroom complicity.

Ann has not lost her moral compass. She just acts out from a chemical imbalance in her brain. No one takes her to a doctor. That's only for those who are ill and feel pain. Even though Ann's increased sexual activity is coupled with other symptoms of bipolar, those who love and work with her close their eyes to her chaotic explosions. Ann likes it that way.

Spiritual Reflection

Forgiveness is not for sissies. Forgiving another for minor hurts such as insults, insensitivities and forgetfulness may take several telephone calls, flowers or time. Forgiving another or oneself for deep hurts sometimes seems impossible. Charlie turns to God for answers, relief and hope. He prays, pleads with God and writes letters to an absent Ann. He eventually throws away the letters and holds his tongue in front of the children. Besides this stabbing, brain-piercing, ripped-heart experience for Charlie, he has another burden that emanates from self-loathing. When he focuses on Ann, rage burns like lava in his veins. When he thinks about his own payoff, every muscle in his body becomes rigid. He slaps his hands to his head when he realizes that he is no better than Ann. Charlie turns to scripture and prayer to learn how to forgive both Ann and himself. He knows his mind will store the hurt, betrayal and powerlessness he has experienced over the years. Forgiveness is his goal. Memory cannot be erased.

Jesus was a student of the Old Testament and believed in a gracious and forgiving God. He taught his disciples and the people who would listen to him that forgiveness needs to be both in prayer and action. When the disciples asked Jesus to teach them to pray, it is reported in Luke's gospel that he said, "Pray then in this way" and taught them "The Lord's Prayer." That prayer is about fourteen lines long. Two lines speak to forgiveness: ". . . And forgive us our debts / as we forgive our debtors." Jesus concludes his instruction by responding only to the lines on forgiveness. In the gospel of Mathew, he says to his disciples: "For if you forgive others their trespasses, your heavenly Father will also forgive you; but if you do not forgive others, neither will your Father forgive your trespasses."

Charlie memorized The Lord's Prayer as a child in Sunday school, but reading Jesus' comments after The Lord's prayer disturbs him. He believes his faith requires him to forgive Ann. Now, he must also bring himself into the mix -- he is part of the problem in their relationship. He'd much rather focus on Ann's indiscretions.

Jesus understood the power of forgiveness as a life-changing act of healing. When a robber, prostitute or other "sinner" approached Jesus for healing, he frequently said, "Your sins are forgiven, Go and sin no more." When Charlie read these stories he wept. There was no forgiveness is his heart.

In one story, a religious leader invited Jesus for dinner. An uninvited woman arrived with ointment and water. She wept and her tears fell upon Jesus' feet. She wiped his feet dry with her long hair. Then she kissed his feet and massaged oil onto them. The host turned to Jesus and asked him how he could allow this woman to touch him because she was a "sinner." Jesus answered:

> Do you see this woman? I entered your house; you gave me no water for my feet, but she has bathed my feet with her tears and dried them with her hair. You gave me no kiss; but from the time I came in she has not stopped kissing my feet. You did not anoint my head with oil, but she has anointed my feet with ointment. Therefore, I tell you, her sins, which were many, have been forgiven; hence she has shown great love. But the one to whom little is forgiven, loves little.

Jesus sent the woman on her way with the parting words. "Your sins are forgiven." With Jesus' words, she now possessed a new life. She loved. She received forgiveness.

Charlie struggles with this story. He wants Ann to ask him for forgiveness, maybe even beg for it. But the kicker for Charlie is that Jesus ended his conversation with his host by pointing out the consequences of a hardened heart. The religious leader heard that acts of love gave forgiveness; judgment fueled punishment.

Charlie ponders, "I love Ann and do many acts of love. Why then has forgiveness eluded me? What am I missing in this story?" He stands up and pushes his chair back; it falls over. He heads upstairs too frustrated to think. Days later, the quiet of the basement calls to him. There he sits in a corner, his Bible front and center. He flips the pages until his eyes find the word "forgiveness." He finds it pretty easily. This disturbs him.

In the gospel of Mathew, a disciple asked Jesus if a person sinned against him, should he forgive the sinner more than seven times. Jesus stared at the disciple and said, "Not seven times, but I tell you, seventy-seven times." Charlie flees the basement and looks for a cloth. In the midst of a cloud of dust, he remembers another biblical lesson from Sunday school: Don't judge others. "That's for sure," he mumbles. He retrieves his Bible, decides to carry it upstairs, and in better light reads Jesus' words in Matthew 7:

> Do not judge, so that you may not be judged. For with the judgments you make you will be judged and the measure you give will be the measure you get. Why do you see the speck in your neighbor's eye, but do not notice the log in your own eye?

> Or how can you say to your neighbor, "Let me take the speck out of your eye," while the log is in your own eye? You hypocrite, first take the log out of your own eye and then you will see clearly to take the speck out of your neighbor's eye.

Charlie doesn't like what he is reading. But he knows Ann has made many mistakes and hurt their relationship and her relationship with her children. Charlie prays for help.

Charlie's Prayer

Dear God. I read your words. I wrestle with them. Who hasn't? I know I do not sit in this place alone. Month upon month I bend between rage, hurt and love. I can't change Ann, nor can the kids. Just this truth makes me mad. You would think her love for us would be greater than whatever she does. I can't seem to walk through this mess with a clear head. I am paralyzed with my inability to forgive. My strength wanes. I need your help. I trust you. I lean upon your grace. I am so tired. Amen.

CHILD

The Story

I keep my scary stories to myself; I don't even tell my sister. We have two dads; one we call Daddy, the other Papa. This arrangement may seem unusual to some. A few of my friends think my family is *weird*. Others call it *cool*. I call it *difficult*. Don't get me wrong. I love both my dads and I know they love me. They attend all my school stuff as well as my art exhibits (mostly posted on the walls outside my classroom!). They framed one picture and sent a few to my grandparents and my aunt and uncle. I like my life, the one most people see. Once in awhile, everything falls apart, though. Papa calls these times "shallow shadows." I privately name them "scary, ugly, no-good times." I don't know when one begins, I just know five things happen: Daddy, who has bipolar, acts strange; Daddy and Papa really go after each other; I get sent to my aunt and uncle's; I get scared; the family doesn't talk about these times.

The last "scary, ugly, no-good time" happened just a few months ago. All I remember is that Daddy spent more time at home, lounged around the house, screamed awful words to Papa, and did not want me or my sister around. Aunt Jane and Uncle Greg came to get us and my dog, Gypsy. The same old, same old. I like visiting them, though, because they let Gypsy sleep with me and I still get to go to my regular school. But often our stay is too long.

Sometimes these "scary, ugly, no-good times" feel fun at first. Last time, Daddy showed me big colored pictures of cabinets, decks and gazebos he had built for real fancy houses and cooked all our favorite foods. My sister ordered special pizza, root-beer floats and Daddy's specialty, miniature truffles. I asked for cheese goulash (no green peppers, please), cotton candy and quinoa (I just learned that word) chili salad. Gypsy got pizza, too. Papa quietly said he would eat the leftovers. Even though it was a school night, Daddy brought home an armful of movies we could watch until we fell asleep. The other great thing was that he said we could stay home from school and watch movies, go to the zoo, and later stop by to watch him play "out-of-the-park" softball. At the ballpark, Daddy yelled from the outfield, "Watch me." He caught the ball and put on a dance. In the dugout, he paced until it was his turn to bat. His teammates yelled, "Start us off." He slammed a home run. He made the game fun for me, but I could tell that some of his teammates didn't like him. Now I wonder what fun things will happen tonight!

Not much. It is now evening; Pappa has returned. I escape to my room. Daddy and Papa begin a private conversation. In a short time they scream and use awful words with each other. Daddy slams the door on his way out of the house and then doesn't return for several days. I was scared, real scared. We all were. At these "scary, ugly, no-good times," I don't like my family. I am scared of both Daddy and Papa. I just want them to stop arguing and get along. I think I must be doing something to make this happen.

Comments on the Story

Bipolar disorder makes kids scared. As in other families experiencing multiple stressors -- divorce, physical abuse, death of a pet, visits from relatives that go badly -- children wonder if they caused the problem. Some families, though, have a strong support system; kids can be sheltered from the worst dynamics. Papa knew the warning signs of Daddy's bipolar disorder and had trusted relatives who would take the children and try to maintain support and stability until the episode subsided. Many children, however, experience the trauma of major mood swings without outside resources. When a parent exhibits unwarranted grandiosity and anger, impaired judgment and other manic symptoms, or the crash of crushing depression, children need a safe haven. Support people can make the difference in a family staying together as well as trying hard to ease the children's fear and extreme negative judgment of the person with bipolar disorder.

Many times relatives simply get tired of holding up a family in crisis. They choose -- for the welfare of the children -- to go to the courts and ask for custody. This action pains everyone and takes a toll on all involved. In some families, the person with bipolar has only one choice: to explain to the children his brain-chemical problem. That most likely will put the family into chaos. This less-than-desirable approach places the children as the caretakers. A worse scenario, common in the bipolar community, is a family in crisis. Each person just lives through it. Such a situation may result in a fractured family. All the above scenarios get more complicated when families face other stressors, such as poverty, unemployment, financial insecurity, multiple health issues and isolation.

Spiritual Reflection

Fear of a demon-possessed person occurs throughout the Bible. In the Old Testament, one of the clearest examples is that of King Saul, the first king of the Israelites. The people begged God to give them a ruler like all the surrounding communities. God heard their pleas and chose Saul. The people celebrated. Saul felt God's call. He married and fathered sons. But his mind became disturbed and soon he trusted no one, not even his son Jonathan. King Saul became paranoid and filled with rage, stirring fear in the people. No one could approach him, least of all Jonathan and his best friend, David. Eventually, Saul became so mentally ill that he had to be removed from his throne. God chose David to be the next king.

In the New Testament, Jesus found a man living outside his community, chained to rocks. Daily he roared at imaginary beings and yanked at his chains until blood ran down his arms. Jesus approached him, touched his body and the man was freed from bondage and mental torture. He felt the healing and pleaded with Jesus that he might go with him. But Jesus replied that his best work would be to tell his community over and over again what God did for his life and can do for others.

No one is so sick, that God shuns him or her. Rather, God welcomes everyone into the fold.

Child's Prayer
Dear Lord Jesus. I love my parents but they need to be different. I sometimes feel so alone and scared because they act real mad. I don't like having to move away, not knowing when I can return. I love my aunt and uncle; that's not the problem. Maybe I am. I remember a

picture of you surrounded by little children. You look like you care about each of them. Can I be one of those kids? Not forever, but just for those "scary, ugly, no-good times?" I want to be a good kid. I want my Daddy and Papa around me and happy every day. Can you do this for my sister and me? Gypsy too? Amen.

LEAH

The Story

With her new GPS -- a gift from her nervous parents -- Leah sets off for Seattle. Her heart palpitates with excitement, and a cell phone lays next to her for safety. Doctoral degree in hand, Leah drives the thousand miles to her first teaching job. Behind her are all her support systems: her family, lifelong friends from the city, precious relationships in her church. In the past weeks, her high-risk choice to move has elevated Leah's anxieties and driven her to sleepless nights and interminable sessions on the Internet. She has searched out every Seattle neighborhood for affordable apartments, studied statistics about the city, identified tourist attractions and reached out to her never-met cousin.

Leah's U-Haul is filled with more books than furnishings or clothes. She's ready to work. Success in this job will provide her with several ladder-climbing career opportunities. But first she must "rock" when she meets the chairman of the English department one week from today. She is professionally and psychologically prepared to meet him as well as the other faculty members. She thinks she will be the youngest professor in her department.

The week passes and the meeting with her chairman goes well, except that he informs Leah that an additional class has been added to her load. She now will need to prepare for three classes plus a seminar. The chairman also mentions several social events within the department she will be expected to attend in order, he says, "to build department cohesiveness." Leah isn't comfortable with these added responsibilities.

Over the next few weeks, she grows even more anxious, which leads to her poor preparation for the added class. Additionally, at the first social event, everyone else comes coupled. Leah feels out of place.

At first she speaks regularly to her family and friends, but these conversations wane as Leah feels less secure. She begins hiding from colleagues out of fear that they will notice her growing restlessness. During one seminar, she snaps at a student for offering frivolous comments. The following week during a lecture, she approaches a student who has fallen asleep and pounds his desk.

Leah's erratic behaviors escalate and students begin complaining to other faculty members. Concerned, the department chairman calls her to his office and questions her about her first few months of teaching. When Leah leaves, she knows that she must take four actions: she must *not* call her parents or friends; she needs to find a doctor who will prescribe sleeping pills; she must find a yoga class; and she must call her pastor "back home."

Leah's performance continues to deteriorate. She makes no friends. She has little interest in food. And she doesn't sleep well. Finally, she makes an appointment with an internist. The doctor takes a family history, listens to her complaints and speaks to her about the possibility of being bipolar. Leah nearly laughs out loud. She just needs more sleep, she says. The doctor provides her with a mood-stabilizing medication and suggests that she return in three weeks. He also gives her a pamphlet on bipolar disorder and a clinic's emergency telephone number. Leaving the appointment, Leah is angry with the doctor for suggesting she might be mentally ill. Nevertheless, that evening she takes the medication.

In a few weeks, Leah's classes barely improve but she feels better. She returns to the doctor. Leah reports that her life is improving and they decide to continue the mood-disorder medication. The doctor asks her to return in six weeks. In the meantime, Leah's pastor calls and she asks him that their conversation be held in confidence. The pastor agrees. Leah speaks openly about her fears, her anxieties and even her doctor appointments. He listens attentively and suggests that she could benefit from spending time with a spiritual director he knows in the Seattle area. Leah makes an appointment to do that. She puts yoga on the back burner and limits contact with her parents and friends to letters.

Comments on the Story
Leah was scared. Even her Ph.D. orals could not compare to the terror she now feels. At first, she denied that she might have bipolar disorder. After all, her life back home seemed normal. She experienced a few weird times but everyone agreed that the stress of school caused those episodes. Now, without support and with greater demands and expectations of her performance and a growing sense of being an outsider, Leah's behavior warranted the consideration of a bipolar diagnosis. Leah couldn't believe she could be "crazy," even though the discussion with her doctor made sense and the medication improved her quality of life. And the pamphlet did describe many of her feelings and behaviors. She made an appointment to see the spiritual director only because her pastor urged her to do so. What good would this visit be, she wondered. "Probably my time would be better spent working more hours preparing for my classes and that miserable seminar," she thought.

Spiritual Reflection
Upon sitting on an earth-toned cushy chair in the spiritual director's room, Leah looks around and sees no Bibles, commentaries or crosses. Rather, quotations are artistically placed on each wall. She notices the softer lighting, the stones in the center of a draped table and a peaceful person sitting across from her. Leah is surprised to find that she feels relatively relaxed.

When the spiritual director asks what is happening in her life, Leah finds herself speaking her truth: She has been diagnosed with bipolar disorder and she feels uncomfortable with this information. Then, to her amazement, she utters the words, "I feel like such a failure and have so much shame." After listening to Leah's story, the director responds, "You have had quite a journey. I will be with you on your path as you move forward. Take a stone from this dish and remember the Ark of the Covenant rested on them, Jesus stood upon the rocks at the Galilean Sea, and David took a stone to defeat a treacherous giant. Let's talk again in two weeks." Leah agrees and makes the appointment.

Leah descends the stairs and notices a variety of painted canvases strung together by wire wrapped with rainbow-colored ribbons. On each canvas a Psalm verse has been written in calligraphy. Such beauty attracts her and she slowly reads each one. She feels calm. For the first time in a long time she feels God next to her.

She reads the first verse of Psalm 4:1: "Answer me when I call, O God of my right! You gave me room when I was in distress. Be gracious to me, and hear my prayer." The next canvas has these words etched in charcoal gray: "Be not far from me, for trouble is near and there is no one to help." Leah feels those words from Psalm 22 best speak to her conflicted life. A lime-green canvas holds Psalm 25: "Show me your ways, Yahweh! Teach me your paths! Lead me in your truth, and teach me. For you are the God of my salvation. I wait all the day long for you." She hopes the conversations with her spiritual director will set her on the path that is her truth. Her eye gaze upon the citron canvas that records Psalm 35: "(O God), do not be far from me." That will be her mantra.

Leah continues to meet with her spiritual director. Appointment by appointment, she is able to accept that her bipolar disorder caused her incalculable embarrassing times from which she suffered deep shame. With a better understanding of her medical condition, she realizes that others with the same disorder have behaved in similar ways. That being so, Leah turns to the difficult work of self-forgiveness. Ripe memories of shameful times, like echoes, make her efforts to achieve wholeness challenging. Without engaging in daily spiritual practices, Leah believes she would be saddled with perpetual regrets.

Spiritual Director's Prayer

Daily I pray to you, oh my God, for wisdom to hear your people's stories and to walk with them toward your loving kindness and steadfastness. I see your healing touch upon hurting, angry and disenfranchised people. Leah joined my heart today. May I be fully with her. Strengthen me to tend to her wounds however she may speak them. She tells me of her shame and anger at being born with this disability. Once she felt whole; now with bipolar disorder she believes herself to be incurably sick. Give me a gentle spoon to stir the hope you freely give that rests deep within her. With your wisdom, mother her to stand on Holy Ground. I see her eyes resting on your Psalms. Plant them in her very being. May your ancient words pierce the darkness of her shame and anger and bring it to the light of fluttering butterflies. Thank you for the blessing of Leah to me. Amen.

On more than one occasion, the Dalai Lama has been asked to define "spirit," a foundational principle of the major religions of the world. He explained that if one were to invite representatives of the ten largest religions for a summit to define the word, the group would be unsuccessful because "spirit" is such a complex religious term.

Consulting a dictionary to seek clarity about the word, which is in most people's vocabulary, reinforces that complexity. On Dictionary.com, for example, thirty definitions for "spirit" appear. They can be placed in two categories. The first, and larger, encompasses "secular" meanings. Examples include shedding light on a person (kind spirit), describing an activity (spirited game), or describing another being (horse with the spirit to win).

The second category on the website uses Webster's Dictionary as its primary source. Several definitions mirror those listed in the previous paragraph, but Webster's includes more detailed definitions oriented toward religious use of "spirit." Three of these definitions are:

(1) Life, or living substance, considered independently of corporeal existence; an intelligence conceived of apart from any physical organization or embodiment; vital essence, force, or energy, as distinct from matter.

(2) The intelligent, immaterial and immortal part of man; the soul, in distinction from the body in which it resides; the agent or subject of vital and spiritual functions, whether spiritual or material.

(3) Air set in motion by breathing; breath; hence, sometimes, life itself.

This third definition leads into the biblical discussion of "spirit."

In the three major western religions -- Christianity, Islam and Judaism – "spirit" is a common word. An old word. A wisdom word. "Spirit" appears in the first lines of the Jewish and Christian bibles and is found in several places in the Qur'an. In both Jewish and Christian scriptures, "spirit" is translated in Hebrew as "Ruah." Like many Hebrew words, multiple meanings exist. For example, the translation of "Ruah" can mean spirit, wind or breath. This explanation is helpful because Ruah appears in the first sentence of both bibles and is repeated several times in the creation stories.

The first story is that of Adam and Eve, dated around 2500 BCE and passed down in oral tradition. In this story, God made the earth and the heavens but nothing was alive because it had not rained. When God wanted to fashion a human, a stream came forth and the earth flourished. To create a human, God gathered particles of the earth's surface, formed the first human, and blew the "breath-wind-spirit" (Ruah) into shape, and the first human, Adam, was brought into existence. Later, God, knowing that Adam needed a partner, created Eve using a rib of Adam. Thus God's breath created Adam and Adam's rib created Eve, which allowed God's living breath to pass to Eve.

The second creation story is dated during King David's reign, the tenth century BCE. In this story, the "spirit-wind" (Ruah) of God hovers over the "formless and void"; nothing has yet been created. God alone calls forth in six days the universe, light, darkness, water, earth, animals, plants and sea creatures. Each part of the universe is necessary for sustaining humanity. And God says, "Let us make humanity in our image and likeness . . . and in the image of God he created them; male and female he created them." With God's breath (Ruah), all living things came into being.

In just over four verses, scripture records that God uses Ruah to create humanity as well as a perfect world. All that has come into being has done so by the "spirit" of God. God, therefore, lies deep within each person. Creator and creature, like parent and child, are authentically intimate yet separate entities. With these creation stories, the nature of God is central. People's responses to the spirit of God now become spirituality -- one's expression of the "breath-spirit-wind" of God.

What concerns us here is how people with bipolar disorder and their various support people imagine God: What is the nature of God? How does God fit into each person's life?

Members of the bipolar community describe God in very different ways. Some believe that God does not exist and, therefore, God's nature is irrelevant. At one time, these individuals might have talked of God or a Higher Power, but given so many treacherous walks in lonely places, the nature of God has become irrelevant. They now believe that if God existed, life would have been different for them. If they felt that some being was compassionate or kind or liking, maybe then a belief in some spiritual entity might exist for them.

Other members of the bipolar community believe in God. Their perceptions, as well as their experiences, inform them that God "comes and goes." God is more present to them when moods are stable and less so when they feel overwhelmed by the damage that bipolar episodes have done to relationships, work environments and their own self-regard. At these times, turning to God for solace may be more difficult than turning to God in anger and yelling out, "Where were you when. . . ?" God matters, but once again the person with bipolar disorder doesn't feel "good enough," not even a little bit. The nature of God turns out to mirror the nature of the disorder: up and down, in and out.

For some people with bipolar disorder, God is the friend who walks by their side and sits in the dark room where they are hiding from the light. God waits. These people believe that if they get into a really tight spot, God will be there also. God never leaves, waivers or shuns. For others, belief of God relates to one's belief of Satan. For someone in the bipolar community, God's nature becomes a warrior, as does Satan. The story places God and Satan within each person's body. They continually fight for dominance. The person's role is to endure this war in order to give God the opportunity to defeat Satan.

Throughout the creation stories, God assures all people that they are "good." It would be is impossible to find a word, phrase or image within the stories that indicates otherwise. The picture of God gathering dust and holding it so the wind could not scatter any particles seems impossible. Yet God breathed into this fragile mass and created a human. Both male and female were created as equals. God did not prefer one sex over the other, or one born disease-free over one with a disease.

Whether one thinks that God is dead, sleeping, way out in the universe or intimately present, the issue of suffering must be addressed. Those people born with a disability they did nothing to acquire and who live with its ruinous attacks have the right to ask, "Why me, God?" And they deserve an answer.

Respected theologians suggest that suffering is part of the human experience and great wisdom results from suffering. As some people with the disorder may agree, the vulnerability to the attacks of bipolar have given them a level of compassion toward others. Nonetheless, given a choice of living with the disorder or being free of it, many likely would choose to be free of the disorder. The gift of deeper compassion is not worth the pain of too many relationships destroyed, too many jobs lost, frequent money worries and disrespect.

The theologians who argue that suffering is one's lot in life might say that having bipolar disorder was just the bad luck of the draw. A person must endure this suffering for the heavenly rewards after death. But for the person with bipolar, enduring severe episodic bouts of bipolar may be seen as too high a price for a place in heaven. They ask, "What kind of God would offer a lifetime of hell in exchange for an eternal heaven?" And if this is the equation, then this God is not one to be worshipped or praised.

Still other theologians hold that the creation stories set the stage to envision God as one who created humanity and called it "good." God blessed humanity and gave people all they need for lives of wholeness and abundance. With this view, living with bipolar has nothing to do with God. Maybe it's hereditary, maybe it's post-traumatic stress, maybe it's just the luck of the draw. God does not toss out some people and give others comfort and coziness.

Ultimately, then, the answer to "Why me, God?" comes from an individual's point of view. How one learned about God, currently views God, and what one expects of God provide the answer to this personal question.

From my work with people with mental-health-illness issues, spiritual questions arise after the primary questions -- symptom expressions, relationship stories, problems with consequences from the disorder -- have been discussed. Spiritual conversations begin when the anxiety of the person's life loosens its grip. Most of the time people are either angry at God and the church or they rely on God for presence, patience and answers. From whatever position they hold, discussions can go long into the night. People hunger for peace with God even if that means discounting the presence of God. So far in my work, I have yet to meet a person who believes "spirit" is non-existent. Some just call it love. And that is a fine answer because love is what God is all about.

My Story

At age 41, I applied to seminary. Following a few biographical questions on the application was my most-feared question: "Why do you want to attend seminary?" I wrote, "To figure out if there is a God." Weeks later, when I received my acceptance letter, I decided the United Theological Seminary of the Twin Cities desperately needed students. It also occurred to me that at this ecumenical seminary, one's questions clearly mattered.

When I walked into my first class -- New Testament – I was nine months pregnant. In order to pass the class, I would need my baby to lay motionless and silent for 90 minutes and a handful of students to share their notes. The first assignment gave me great anxiety. I needed to write an informational piece -- no more than two pages -- about my faith formation from the Bible, people who influenced my thinking and experiences that enhanced or distracted from my journey. With a bit of hyperventilating, I found comfort only in the length of the assignment. After a couple of days, however, I identified three pivotal spiritual/religious experiences.

My first concept of God was a common image of the almighty Father. God, wearing a white robe and with flowing white hair, had a face carved from centuries of anger and judgment. I didn't need this God. Life was tough enough without the demands of worshiping such a distant, scary figure. I would make it on my own.

My parents were C and E -- Christmas and Easter -- congregants. We were a family without two coins to rub together. One December, the church decided to help us through the Christmas season. The pastor dropped by with two bags of food; everyone except Dad greeted him. The pastor spoke quietly to Mom, handed her the groceries and, before leaving, offered a prayer. My young ears heard words that told me he did not like our family. I may have been only eight or nine, but I felt his disdain. I did not like him. Later in the week, my dad's union delivered a turkey. The note read, "Merry Christmas from your union members." No judgments came with this gift. We ate with gratitude.

My second important experience with God came a few years later. No matter how my parents felt about "our" church, I needed to get baptized and learn the teachings of the Lutheran church. I attended classes and in a few months I would be baptized (I wouldn't go to Hell) and confirmed (I would be a believer). Given those momentous events, I expected God to show himself to me. I waited at the communion rail long after the parents and kids had gone downstairs for refreshments. No God. I waited some more. No God. Finally, I walked away feeling shamed; obviously I was not wanted.

The third formative experience held mystery for me. Even with my feelings of inadequacy, most Sundays I walked more than an hour to attend church or, rather, to be out of the house. A few blocks from my church, there was a quaint outdoor Catholic prayer station. I never saw any staff or visitors or even curious neighbors. The sidewalk ran along one side of the structure. A prayer railing with soft kneeling benches arched around the entire depictions of the Stations of the Cross. I didn't understand much that was presented, but I was drawn in and felt a calmness -- a feeling rarely known in my everyday life. Some Sundays I would arrive at church late because I had spent a few extra minutes kneeling and studying the "Stations" artwork. Looking back, I concluded that these rich moments had birthed my first blush with the mystery of faith.

In high school, college, graduate school and employment, I spent my time being a person with anxiety and bipolar disorder, and dealing with the consequences of several sexual assaults. I was too busy being miserable to hang out with God. I was barely able to hang onto myself. I tried to be happy. Sometimes I was too happy.

I focused on college, career and growing-up. This last part gave me the most difficulty. I read a ton of self-help books. I attended workshops on the five stages of the development of the self, the seven stages of self actualization, the hard work of forgiveness, the identity and power of shame, the feminist movement and countless other topics to internalize self-worth. I kept bumping into God and then, like the "bumper car" rides at a fair, turning away, only to bump into God again.

But on the day my daughter took her first breaths and the nurse placed her on my bare and flabby stomach, I heard God's words in my head. And in that moment I realized that I needed to know whether those words came from some chemical after-birth reaction or God. Today, the answer is clear and held deep within me. God's presence at my "birthing chair" did more than open wide my heart. I experienced God luring me to search, to find and to accept the God who I no longer needed to fear or ignore. It was then I understood that if I listened to my spirit, I would be with God.

About the author

During the time I was working for my bachelor's degree, the university sponsored a trip to the Soviet Union. Upon arriving at the border, I looked out the bus window and glared at the soldiers carrying machine guns. Later on the trip, we went down into the catacombs to view more than fifty preserved bodies from before World War I. The sight of skeletons with see-through clothing turned my stomach. When I emerged from the dark and moist pathways, I vomited. For the first time, I had a vivid picture of a culture very different from my own. I was eager to explore others.

Given this new passion, I attended the University of Minnesota for a Master's degree in intercultural communication and another passion of mine, the dynamics of small-group communication. To fulfill the intercultural communication requirements, I decided to travel to eastern, central and south Africa. In Tanzania, I was introduced to many different rituals, family structures, thatched-roof mud houses and the birthing chair. The chair captivated me as I imagined thousands of women giving birth using this ancient method. I was compelled to buy one and carried it on my back until I arrived home. I have moved many times over the decades, and that chair has always been wrapped in a blanket and placed in a safe spot in my car.

After my Master's, I held several jobs in social services. Working as the executive director of one the largest women's centers in the country challenged every skill I had honed. The center operated with part-time staff, volunteers and collective decision-making. Each year it provided more than one thousand women with chemical-dependency, mental-health and legal services. In two and a half years, I raised more than two million dollars. Today I believe my successes can be attributed to several hypomanic episodes.

Drawing on all that I had learned from the women using the center's services, I accepted a position as a Legislative Assistant to a U.S. senator. I was responsible for nineteen areas, all in human services. I met with experts, organization leaders, advocacy groups and individuals interested in a specific bill. I also spoke to groups ranging from small non-profits to Fortune 500 companies. Health-care reform, including mental health, consumed the greatest amount of my time.

In 1981, President Carter established a Commission on Mental Health. The commission determined that mental-health services across the country varied greatly, from minimum to inadequate. The commission urged Congress to pass legislation that would establish quality mental-health services in each state. I guided the senator to not only cast an "Aye" vote on the bill but also to advocate for its passage with his colleagues. I believe the passage of this legislation paved the way for the inclusion of mental-health services in the Americans With Disabilities Act of 1990.

After years of work in the non-profit and public sectors, in 1983 I decided to enter the private sector. I wanted to continue my education as to the perception of people with mental-health illnesses as well as learn about the services larger companies provided employees suffering with chronic illnesses.

During my corporate years, I started a family. Three children in five years required my full attention. Every day seemed to bring more homework, more sports, more teacher-parent conferences, more school volunteering and less time with my spouse and female friends. Stress alerted me to noticeable mood changes. I was frightened. I needed help. I began attending Al-Anon meetings and found that the focus on a Higher Power intrigued me. I didn't know my convictions about God. I thought I should, so in 1988 I decided to attend seminary.

Over the next four years, I was required to complete two internships. My first choice placed me in a "safe house" for women escaping a variety of dire circumstances. I was shocked to learn of cults that included barbaric treatment of women that left them with physical scars, psychotic episodes and nightmares. Two of the survivors shared stories with me – stories far beyond my comprehension.

My second internship was nine months with one of the largest African American Baptist churches in Minnesota. I learned a new church culture. I learned about the power of preaching, music and prayer. And I learned how the church helped people in distress. In this book, the story of Kisha reflects some of what I learned.

I needed the music, the joy and the resulting strength that this internship provided. The year was 1991, the year I learned I had bipolar disorder. The next year, I graduated and was ordained as a minister – a support person for suffering people. I felt inadequate, overwhelmed and scared.

But I needed to work to help heal others and myself. I accepted a three-year position to hold a weekly noon service in an enclosed downtown garden. Frequently, after the short service, people would seek out my counsel about serious issues facing them. Mental-health issues topped the list. It topped my list, too. I regularly took my medicine and attended support groups. Yet no medicine had alleviated the dark depression that daily accompanied me. My job performance stunk. I asked God, "If you wanted me to be this minister, why this depression?" And I wondered, "If I asked the senior pastor for help, would I lose my job?"

No answers came to me. People in my support groups walked through murky waters. How did they think about God? If a person in the group brought up God, it was with a destructive belief that Satan lived within him or with anxious confusion. I believed answers existed. I wanted to wrestle with the questions. This desire led me to work for a doctorate and focus on God, mental health and spirituality. I studied more about bipolar disorder and read numerous books on the nature of God and suffering.

What I have learned, my comfort in sharing my own experiences, and the need for God to be in the equation of healing allow me to give many speeches, lead workshops, consult with organizations and offer coaching and counseling. I spend a great deal of time on hope, healing, God's presence in suffering, shame, the effects of bipolar disorder on relationships and specific concerns from support people. In return, on evaluation forms people express their gratitude that they feel "sane" -- not alone, shamed or abandoned by God. I am honored to be part of so many people's lives.

For obvious privacy reasons, not to mention the intrusiveness of the Internet, I decided to use a pseudonym – Dr. Kay Bernard -- in my professional work. Let me be perfectly clear: When it comes to my life with bipolar and other mood disorders, I am an open book. When it comes to my family, friends and personal interest, however, I am a private person.

Website -- www.bipolarspiratualhealing.com

E-mail – drkaybernard@bipolarspiratualhealing.com

Made in the USA
Charleston, SC
12 April 2016